Praise for
Philosophy Camps for Youth

"Bursting with insight and wisdom that comes from experience, *Philosophy Camps for Youth* offers a compelling and comprehensive map to guide inquiry into the practicalities and rewards of establishing and working with a young community of philosophical inquirers. The range of contributors celebrates the flexibility of philosophical inquiry to suit any local context, and the sample lesson plans and post-camp feedback serve to demonstrate just how valuable it is to give learners a leading role in exploring the curious world of ideas. A heart-warming and hopeful read that will inspire philosophers and educators alike. If there was a copy of this in every library, there'd be a philosophy camp in every town!" —**Marelle Rice, director, The Thinker's Midwife; director, Philosophy Ireland**

"*Philosophy Camps for Youth* is an inspirational volume. It is the absolutely necessary companion piece to *Growing Up with Philosophy Camp*, because here we learn the logistics of creating a camp from the ground up, how to actually 'do philosophy' with plenty of nuts-and-bolts exercises, and (perhaps best of all) we also get to hear directly from the students and parents about their personal transformations. This book is a sustained refutation of common tropes about the uselessness of the humanities precisely because it blends the mind-stretching 'star-gazing' of philosophers like Plato with the practical experiences of professors, university students, parents, and the campers themselves. It is also a gift to democracy, because it gives each of us the tools to create our *own* community of thinkers that can endure beyond a summer camp. Plato's Academy is indeed dead: long live the Academy!" —**Stefan Dolgert, associate professor, political science, Brock University**

"In an age of unprecedented access to information and unprecedented vulnerability to disinformation, it is important to help young people live examined lives. Philosophy camps are a valuable resource in this effort, and Claire Katz's book is essential reading for anyone looking to run one. What a treasure!" —**Paul C. Taylor, W. Alton Jones Professor of Philosophy and department chair, Vanderbilt University**

"Claire Katz's new volume on the what, why, and how of pre-college philosophy camp offers a much-needed reminder that philosophy is something that we do with other people. Importantly, it goes a step further, showing us that these people must be neither holders of advanced degrees nor minimally of college age. Through a number of essays by academic professionals, teachers, students, and camp participants alike, it becomes clear that philosophy camp is not only a bright spot of genuine intellectual and emotional growth amid a landscape of modern childhood strewn with entertainment and resume-building 'activities' but a way young people can, and do, discover their identity, their agency, their personhood—and, importantly, those of others. It is a place where youth can be properly 'corrupted' to see a different future for themselves than they might have otherwise imagined. And it is in such a setting that they can discover that thinking through some of life's most difficult problems can be less scary and more inviting when done in open, generous, and accepting communities. I must say that I very much wish that my introduction to philosophy began earlier than it in fact did, at the kind of place that Professor Katz, and all the contributors, bring to life on the pages of this important book." —**Anna Gotlib, JD, PhD, associate professor, philosophy, Brooklyn College CUNY**

"In *Philosophy Camps for Youth*, the rest of the profession discovers what the state of Texas has known for years: Claire Katz's formula for engaging pre-college youth in philosophical inquiry has the potential to change the scope of higher education for the next half century. Katz makes communities of inquiry between philosophers and youth accessible even to those who are new to teaching middle and high schoolers. Perhaps more important, the camp models described by Katz and the other contributors provide a map for philosophers who are keenly interested in philosophy's future in academia. By following their lead, we can broaden our pedagogical mission to include those outside of the university and to create new inquirers who will become the thought-and-ethics leaders throughout our institutions, regions, and industries." —**Jill Hernandez, dean, College of Arts and Humanities, Central Washington University**

"Claire Katz, a leading figure in the pre-college philosophy movement, has compiled the ultimate how-to guide for successfully organizing philosophy camps. *Philosophy Camps for Youth* should become a foundational resource for all those currently or aspiring to work at the intersection of philosophy and K-12 education." —**Darryl De Marzio, PhD, professor, foundations of education, The University of Scranton**

"In this volume, Claire Katz, a recognized leader in the P4C movement, brings together an excellent assembly of contributors who discuss the nuts and bolts of developing and running a philosophy camp for youth. This collection will be indispensable for anyone thinking about engaging in this important and increasingly popular enterprise." —**Matthew Meyer, associate professor, philosophy, The University of Scranton; faculty director, Slattery Center for Humanities**

The *Big Ideas for Young Thinkers Book Series* brings together the results of recent research about pre-college philosophy. There has been sizable growth in philosophy programs for young people. The book series provides readers with a way to learn about all that is taking place in this important area of philosophical and educational practice. It brings together work from around the globe by some of the foremost practitioners of philosophy for children. The books in the series include single-author works as well as essay collections. With a premium placed on accessibility, the book series allows readers to discover the exciting world of pre-college philosophy.

Philosophy Camps for Youth

Everything You Wanted to Know about Starting, Organizing, and Running a Philosophy Camp

Edited by Claire Elise Katz
Series edited by Thomas E. Wartenberg

ROWMAN & LITTLEFIELD
Lanham • Boulder • New York • London

Published by Rowman & Littlefield
An imprint of The Rowman & Littlefield Publishing Group, Inc.
4501 Forbes Boulevard, Suite 200, Lanham, Maryland 20706
www.rowman.com

6 Tinworth Street, London SE11 5AL, United Kingdom

Copyright © 2021 by Claire Elise Katz

All rights reserved. No part of this book may be reproduced in any form or by any electronic or mechanical means, including information storage and retrieval systems, without written permission from the publisher, except by a reviewer who may quote passages in a review.

British Library Cataloguing in Publication Information Available

Library of Congress Cataloging-in-Publication Available

ISBN 9781475859454 (cloth) | ISBN 9781475859461 (paperback) | ISBN 9781475859478 (epub)

For Dan, Olivia, and Evie
Philosophy companions extraordinaire

Contents

Acknowledgments   xiii

Introduction: The Why and the How of Hosting a Philosophy Camp for Youth   1
Claire Elise Katz

PART I: HOW TO START, ORGANIZE, AND RUN A PHILOSOPHY CAMP   11

1. Observations on the Aggie School of Athens: Running a Philosophy Summer Camp in South Central Texas   13
   Claire Elise Katz

2. Developing a Philosophy Summer Camp at the University of Kentucky   35
   Caroline Buchanan, James William Lincoln, Suraj Chaudhary, Clay Graham, Andrew Van't Land, Lauren K. O'Dell, and Colin Smith

3. The Iowa Lyceum   47
   Landon D. C. Elkind and Gregory Stoutenburg

4. The Philosophy and Critical Thinking (PACT) Summer Camp at Ohio State   61
   James Fritz, Lavender McKittrick-Sweitzer, Justin D'Arms, and Julia Jorati

5	Philosophy Summer Camp: A Philosophical World of Tangible Conversations *Kimberly Arriaga-Gonzalez, Cristina Cammarano, and Jackson Malkus*	77
6	Corrupt the Youth Residential Summer Philosophy Camp: Building a Camp with a Strong Culture *Alex Hargroder and Briana Toole*	87
7	From the Ground Up: Developing a High School Philosophy Camp *Charlie Kurth and Adam Waggoner*	97

PART II: SAMPLE ACTIVITIES AND LESSON PLANS — 105

8	Lesson Plan: Justice and Different Types of Evidence *James Fritz*	107
9	Lesson Plan: How Should Scientists Choose the Best Theory? *Roger Sansom*	113
10	Playing the Hobbes Game at Philosophy Camp *Robert K. Garcia*	121
11	Rational Choice Theory and the Prisoner's Dilemma *Cora Drozd*	127
12	Philosophy, Magic, and Curiosity: Reflections on P4C Texas's 2019 Summer Camp *Michael Portal*	133
13	The If/Then Exercise and the Case for Incorporating P4C into Pre-K Camps and Programs *Charles Royal Carlson*	145
14	Teaching Freire: Philosophy for Children Lesson *Ana Olivares-McFadden*	149

PART III: CAMPER/PARENT OBSERVATIONS — 153

15	Camper and Parent Essays **Aggie School of Athens at Texas A&M University**	155 155

Evelyn Conway	155
Calla Duffield	157
Ellie Hague	160
Mia Paulk	161
E. Grace Sorensen	163
Andrew Sorescu, Alina Sorescu, and Sorin Sorescu	164
Surya Sunkari	166
Iowa	167
Nicholas C. Peters	167
Maeve Ward	168
Christopher C. Peters	169
MOSHI Winter Camp	170
Su-Yin Bouchot	170
PACT Ohio State	171
Ezra Johnson	171
Larada McCreary	172
Shefali Sinha	173
Kevin and Melissa Shoultz	174
Salisbury	176
Sophia Smith	176
Ryan Cadwaller	178
Appendix: Precollege Philosophy Works: Meta-Analysis of the Effectiveness of Philosophy for Children Program on Students' Cognitive Outcomes (Excerpt) *Sijin Yan, Lynne Masel Walters, Zhuoying Wang, and Dr. Chia-Chiang Wang*	181
About the Contributors	193

Acknowledgments

Philosophy Camps for Youth is my second edited book on philosophy camps. The first volume, *Growing Up with Philosophy Camp: How Learning to Think Develops Friendship, Community, and a Sense of Self* (Rowman & Littlefield, 2020), collects a set of chapters on philosophical themes fundamental to and that emerge from philosophy camps for youth. This present collection provides the nuts-and-bolts information and guidance for those who wish to embark on this adventure. If the first book was an attempt to persuade readers with regard to the "why" you should start a camp, *Philosophy Camps for Youth* provides the "how."

With regard to the "how to" of running a philosophy camp, I could not do this successfully without the support of so many people across the campus and in the community. Cynthia Olvera and Amy White in the Texas A&M University Campus for Minors Program ensure that our camp is not only compliant with state and federal laws but also a place where the youth who participate in our camp can flourish. Jamie Bosley, Lauren McAuliffe, and Tom Ellis reserved rooms, processed payments, and kept their sense of humor and welcoming dispositions when the philosophy department was invaded by a crowd of young, aspiring philosophers.

The staff in Public Partnership and Outreach (PPO), Office of the Provost, provided generous funding and staff support. In particular, Robert Bisor, then vice president for PPO, whose initial support and imagination actually brought the camp into existence. Chad Wootton, associate vice president for External Affairs, at Texas A&M, continues to support the Philosophy for

Children program. Martha Green guided us through the first two years, and Janice Meyer provided support following Martha's retirement. Dee Dee Leverett provided not only administrative support but also baked our celebratory cake.

The College of Liberal Arts provided generous funding that allowed the camp to continue beyond the first year. Pam Matthews, dean of the College of Liberal Arts, and Gerianne Alexander, who was then associate dean for research, got us started. Associate dean, Leroy Dorsey, provided guidance and support over the past several years. Melbern G. Glasscock Center for Humanities Research provided supplemental funding for the 2019 camp.

In the community, Rusty Surette, who was a reporter for our local television station, KBTX, invited me to the Focus at Four segment so I could advertise the camp. Chelsea Katz, a staff writer for our local newspaper, *The Eagle*, provided us with great public relations in her stories about our camp. CC Creations created spectacular T-shirts. And two of our local restaurants provided lunches at a discounted rate.

Our camp runs smoothly and our campers return each year because our staff is first-rate. I have never met a more dedicated, talented, and easy-to-work-with group of philosophers. In particular, David Anderson, Patrick Anderson, Charles Carlson, Daniel Conway, Desirae Embree, West Gurley, and Sijin Yan provided consistency and reliability, in addition to lending their philosophical and pedagogical talents.

Texas A&M graduate students, Haley Burke, Ben Faltesek, Victoria Green, and Michael Portal, provided additional philosophical perspectives. Belen Castanon Moreschi and Guillermo Garcia Urena, graduate students in Hispanic Studies (now PhDs), provided a Spanish/English dual-language opportunity for our campers. Our undergraduate volunteers, Cora Drozd, Hannah Philibert, Kenji Blum, Alexa Etheredge, Olivia Conway, Jadyn Driver, Griffin Ford, and Margaret Tran, asked probing questions that kept the dialogue moving.

Over the course of five summers, we have had several guests participate in our camp: my colleagues in philosophy, Chris Menzel, Roger Sansom, and Robert Garcia (now at Baylor); the Confucius Institute at Texas A&M; Kevin O'Sullivan, Rebecca Hankins, and Jeremy Brent at Cushing Library; the magician extraordinaire, Mark Mitton; and the wand-makers at Worthwich. We are grateful for the experiences they provided for our campers.

Acknowledgments

I am indebted to Tom Wartenberg, the series editor, who reached out to me to ask if I would be interested in contributing a book to his new series in precollege philosophy. I wound up with so much material that Tom Koerner, the editor of the press, suggested that I divide the one book into two books. I am grateful for the support that both Tom Koerner and Tom Wartenberg provided for this project. Carlie Wall, and the rest of the staff at Rowman & Littlefield have been a pleasure to work with.

The contributors to this volume have clearly devoted themselves to a labor of love each summer. This book provides guidance not only for how to structure a camp but also for a few activities to get you started. The generosity of those who contributed to this volume is a marker of their generosity as teachers and colleagues. One can see why their philosophy camps have been so successful.

I think I can speak for the staff at all camps when I say that we return each summer because of the campers. It would be an understatement to say how much this experience has transformed us as teachers. We are grateful for the opportunity to spend a week facilitating discussions with them, and I am particularly grateful to have watched so many of them grow up philosophically over the past five summers. Their parents' continued support and encouragement keep us going when we hit those few bumps in the road.

One does not usually think of philosophy as a family activity, but this adventure would not have been nearly as much fun if my family had not joined me on it. My husband, Dan Conway, is a fellow philosopher, colleague, and philosophy camp staff member extraordinaire. Our daughters, who were initially skeptical, not only of philosophy but also of philosophy camp, now look forward to the camp each year. Our elder daughter, a STEM student in college, pursues philosophy with passion and has moved from philosophy camper to philosophy camp facilitator; our younger daughter founded and is the president of the philosophy club at her high school. They teach me every day how to be a better teacher, philosopher, parent, and friend. This book is dedicated to them.

I would like to thank the editors at *Analytic Teaching and Philosophical Praxis* for their permission to reprint an excerpt of "Meta-Analysis of the Effectiveness of Philosophy for Children Programs on Students' Cognitive Outcomes," by Sijin Yan, Lynne Masel Walters, Zhuoying Wang, and Chia-Chiang Wang originally published in Vol. 39/No. 1 (2018).

Introduction

The Why and the How of Hosting a Philosophy Camp for Youth

Claire Elise Katz

Although the pre-college philosophy movement is now more than fifty years old, it is only within the last ten to fifteen years that it has begun to receive the national and international recognition that it deserves from those who do not directly participate in it. A recent phenomenon indicative of both the movement's growth and its recognition is the development of philosophy summer camps for youth. Although a philosophy summer camp may initially seem like a strange way for teens and tweens to spend their time during a summer break, the campers' first-person accounts and the observations made by the staff who work in the philosophy camps suggest otherwise.

Full disclosure—I have an MAT from the Philosophy for Children (P4C) program at Montclair State University, which I completed in 1987. Even doing the master's degree was a risky endeavor at a time when there was very little discussion about interdisciplinarity. The relationship between philosophy and education while intimate is also tense. Until the twentieth century, nearly every philosopher in the history of Western philosophy wrote a treatise on education.

In the twentieth century, very few philosophers wrote explicitly on education, and even when they did, those works were often ignored. One would be hard-pressed to find courses in philosophy of education either in colleges of education or philosophy departments. As a result, the relationship between philosophy and education becomes ever more tenuous. Both disciplines are impoverished from this severed relationship. In particular, philosophy, which became increasingly insular in the academy, loses by not engaging its colleagues in discussions about why philosophy is not only important to a robust education but also a joyful way to approach that education. Yet, even I, who was 100 percent persuaded by the Philosophy for Children program, never imagined a philosophy camp for teens.

In April 2018, Tom Wartenberg, the series editor for *Big Ideas for Young Thinkers*, contacted me about doing a book for his new series. Accepting his offer, I decided to do an edited book on philosophy camps for youth, which would allow for multiple voices to contribute to the volume. I knew of a few philosophy camps in the United States and Canada, but I had no idea of the large number—and yet still not large enough—there were. I contacted the staff for those camps I knew of—and I came across a few more along the way—to see if they wished to contribute to the volume. An embarrassment of riches, I wound up with too much material for one book.

Tom Koerner, the editor of the press, suggested I divide the material into two volumes. So, the one edited book became two edited books. The first book, *Growing Up with Philosophy Camp: How Thinking Develops Friendship, Community, and a Sense of Self* (Rowman & Littlefield, 2020), comprises essays with a theoretical focus. Those essays explored the philosophical nature of friendship and community, philosophy as therapeutic, moral education, and so forth within the context of a philosophy camp for youth.

This current volume, *Philosophy Camps for Youth*, provides the "How to" for those who wish to explore starting, organizing, and running a philosophy camp in their community.

WHAT IS PRE-COLLEGE PHILOSOPHY?

Pre-college philosophy encompasses any philosophy program directed at students in K-12 grades. Most schools—public or private—do not offer philosophy in their curriculum. There are exceptions of course, most notably Catholic schools, which have a long educational tradition of philosophical engagement. Other private schools that focus on a great books tradition also typically include philosophy, although there the focus might be on learning the philosophers and less about engaging in philosophical discussion.

Even with the increased emphasis on Advanced Placement (AP) courses and practically earning enough credits for a college degree before one ever sets foot on a college campus, only recently did the College Board begin offering an exam that resembled something like a test on philosophical thinking. The AP course is difficult to add to the curriculum for a number of reasons including teacher preparation.

Additionally, many people who are in academic philosophy worry about how a philosophy course would be taught in K-12 schools. Would it be reduced to a series of multiple-choice questions about who wrote *The Critique of Pure Reason*? Would students really be able to engage and discuss the existential questions about life—evil, ethics, religion, love, beauty, friendship, and so forth—that concern them? Would it be able to engage difficult and controversial questions, or would it be taught in terms of which philosopher said what and when?

Established in the late 1960s by Matthew Lipman, then a professor of philosophy at Columbia University, the P4C program emerged as an early program in teaching children philosophy—more specifically, the program was geared to engage children in philosophical thinking and discussion.[1] Lipman describes how during the Vietnam era adults were unable to discuss the conflict with cogent arguments rather than emotional pleas.[2]

Lipman concluded that habits of good thinking and good reasoning needed to begin earlier than college, where philosophical reasoning is first introduced to many students. Challenging the prevailing view of children offered not only by twentieth-century thinkers like Piaget but also by philosophers extending as far back as Aristotle, Lipman concluded that not only could children do philosophy, they must do philosophy.

Working with Ann Margaret Sharp, Lipman published a series of children's philosophical novels and teachers' manuals to accompany them. Each novel was aimed at a specific age/developmental group and addressed themes and ideas that were of interest to those ages: philosophy of art, friendship, animals, ethics, political philosophy, the environment, and so forth. Based on Charlie Brown and the philosophies of Dewey and Pierce, the P4C methodology is unique among precollege philosophy programs.

The aim is less about establishing or learning philosophical information than it is about developing a community of inquiry, Sharp's signature contribution to the program, where the members of the community learn to trust each other so that the community becomes self-correcting. If, for example, one member has an idea that logically will not work, that member needs be able to trust the community enough that he/she/they can contribute the idea without being ridiculed. But this community is not supposed to be "anything goes." That is, the individual also needs to trust that the community will respond in a way that helps that participant reflect on their position and correct it if needed.

Respect is understood differently within a philosophical discussion. Here, it is understood not as agreement, but, in fact, as dissent. Within philosophical discourse, respect is often shown to the other participants when one disagrees and helps the others become better thinkers. In this way, the community grows together. The aim is neither for the community members to ultimately think alike nor for them to agree; rather the aim is to help each participant be the best thinker they can be. In so doing, the community members forge friendships based on trust and intellectual companionship, a shared commitment to seeking the truth.

To that end, what Sharp and Lipman (and those who followed) realized was that philosophy if done well contributes to the development of a self. Within the community of inquiry, children and young adults develop agency and personhood. They take responsibility for their ideas and they learn to take responsibility for others by caring about what those in the community think.

WHY PHILOSOPHY SUMMER CAMP?

For as long as philosophy has been around, it has been viewed suspiciously. We need only to look to Socrates, the most famous of philosophers, to see the truth of this claim. Asking too many questions, making people nervous about their claims to expertise, Socrates was kindly asked to drink the hemlock. Like the rest of the humanities, philosophy is viewed by its critics as being simultaneously useless and dangerous. On the one hand, it does nothing. People just sit around and ponder life's big questions. On the other, it is viewed as the means to corrupt the youth, precisely because the youth are questioning the things that they are taught.

These two accusations would have been sufficient to make it difficult to introduce philosophy into K-12 schools. However, the history of Western philosophy did not do its own discipline any favors by claiming repeatedly that children *cannot do* philosophy (Aristotle). Other philosophers, who at least thought children were capable of doing philosophy, argued that children *should not* do philosophy (Rousseau). Given on the one hand, philosophy's nefarious reputation, and on the other hand, its own practitioners dissuading its introduction to the youth, bringing philosophy to the pre-college classroom has not been an easy task.

Philosophy camps provide an alternative path to introduce young people to philosophy and its benefits: analytical reasoning, lively impassioned discussions, and the experience of an intellectual community. For some, philosophy camp supplements activities already present in local schools; for others, a philosophy camp, which is relatively inexpensive, is a way to bring philosophy to pre-college age kids when implementing philosophy into the K-12 school is not an option. The benefit of a philosophy camp is that it is a more relaxed atmosphere, allowing for staff to experiment with activities, topics for discussion, and pedagogical models.

In the philosophy camp that we hosted on Texas A&M's campus, we adopted a modified version of the P4C pedagogy. We aim to sit in a circle (or square). We read the passages aloud together during the camp week rather than have the campers read them at home, assuring that the passages are read. We provide time to reflect on what was just read. We do not always take questions to put on the board, but we do set the agenda by the campers' questions. Through gentle guidance from a facilitator, we dig deeper into the reading, we ask for counterexamples, evidence in the text, reasons for a position, and follow-up questions to push the campers' thinking.

For Lipman, P4C is fundamental to a society that holds dear democratic values—pluralism, minority voices, responsibility for decisions, and so forth. Pam Matthews, a professor of English and the dean of the College of Liberal Arts at Texas A&M, saw something similar in this program when she read a report from a task force assembled by our previous dean that detailed ways that the humanities could gain more visibility. In her words,

> Philosophy for Children—or, more broadly, philosophy for the young and curious who hunger (intellectually) for the historical legacy of philosophy, serious discussion, disciplined thinking, attention to language and argument, and communal problem-solving that might make us collectively stronger—seemed just right for honing the practice of putting democratic principles into action.[3]

Regardless of the method employed, we also see this practice of democracy within the philosophy camp. As you will see from the chapters contributed to this volume, each camp developed its own approach to teaching philosophy. Some used a modified version of P4C, others found innovative ways, for example, artistic creation, to approach philosophical and intellectual engagement. These models are presented as suggestions and we hope that readers will take what they find of interest and of use and then adapt these models to fit the interests of their staff and campers.

BENEFITS OF PRE-COLLEGE PHILOSOPHY

The benefits of engaging with philosophy have long been known by college students who have aspirations to attend law school. With its emphasis on logical reasoning, careful reading, and precise writing, philosophy aids in developing the skills that help one become not only an attractive applicant for law school but also a good lawyer. Yet as I have stated elsewhere, majoring in philosophy solely to develop the skills one needs for law school seems almost antithetical to philosophy, which also asks us to consider what it means to live life authentically.

A student might enter a philosophy classroom—or our philosophy camp—thinking that they are there just to develop a set of skills, but they often leave the classroom a wholly different person. When asked if they might take a philosophy class in college, their answers have changed over the years, but more recently the answers range from yes because it is the only discipline that currently sustains my interest to yes because it teaches me how to come up with ideas that are innovative and original to one camper confessing that philosophy has provided the tools to help him "not sweat the small stuff," while another camper recognized that "philosophy is essential for everyone in order to be a more well-rounded, conscientious, and thoughtful person." What started for many of our campers as either a curiosity or a place their parents thought would help them develop reasoning has morphed into the space where they find an intellectual community that is the lifeblood for adolescents struggling to find meaning in the world they inhabit.

The irony of philosophy not being taught in K-12 public schools is that it might be the one discipline for which young adults hunger intellectually. When students say that they hate school, what they are often saying is that they find school meaningless—not in a technical sense. Not in the we need more skills kind of way but in that grand existential way. Philosophy not only speaks to them on its own but also provides a path into other subjects.

Introduction 7

As one camper indicated, once she was introduced to Plato's Allegory of the Cave, she could not help but see the cave everywhere—in conversations with classmates and in the literary works she was reading for English.

In spite of its reputation, philosophy is far from useless and it is dangerous only if one thinks that thinking for oneself is dangerous. And for those who agree, philosophy camp can be an exhilarating experience for both the facilitators and the campers.

HOW TO START A PHILOSOPHY SUMMER CAMP FOR YOUTH

In the previous volume, *Growing Up with Philosophy Camp*, the contributors explored why one might want to start a philosophy summer camp. Those chapters discussed the development of friendship, community, and a sense of self that if not unique to one's experience in a philosophy is certainly enhanced by it. Our aim in the previous volume was to demonstrate the theoretical implications of being exposed to philosophy in a safe environment.

This volume is dedicated to the nuts and bolts of how to get one started. The chapters contributed to this volume by people who direct or teach in philosophy camps scattered throughout the United States provide a variety of different models. Significantly, no matter what model is used, the effects are nearly the same: campers demonstrate an increase in self-esteem, self-confidence, inquisitiveness, reasoning, and intellectual humility among the philosophy campers.

In other words, whatever model you decide to use, if you pay close attention to the needs and interests of the campers, the skills and interests of the staff, and develop a camp that reflects the values fundamental to philosophy—emphasizing attentive listening, developing good reasoning, supporting passionate but respectful discourse, and so forth—your camp will be successful. The key is to develop a camp with which the staff and campers are comfortable.

As you will see from all of the chapters, there are common features that need to be sorted before getting started:

- What is the aim of your camp? These are just examples:
  - Fun, intellectual activity
  - Skills—improve reasoning ability

- Recruiting students to your campus
- Provide an opportunity for socioeconomically challenged campers to experience a college campus and imagine themselves there
* How many staff members? How many campers?
* What age group will the campers be?
* Will you provide pedagogical training for staff? How will you recruit and what are the qualifications?
* What safety regulations are in place at your college/university/institution?
* How will you recruit campers? Will there be qualifications or an application of some sort?
* What kind of funding do you need? Will you pay staff or is this volunteer only?
* If you need funding, who will provide it?
* How long will the camp day be? Will lunch be provided?
* What will your curriculum look like?
* Where will it be housed or held (On campus? In a library? In a youth center?)?
* Will it be a day camp or residential?

These questions should help you get started as you think about how you want your camp to look. The individual chapters will provide guidance with multiple paths you can take as you address each of these questions. You can find contact information for the various camps included in this volume and *Growing Up with Philosophy Camp* on the resources page of the P4CTexas website.[4] We hope that you will contact us if you need more guidance, advice, suggestions or if you want to share your success.

ORGANIZATION OF THE BOOK

The book is divided into three parts. The first part comprises chapters exploring different philosophy camp models. For example, some camps run all day for one week while some chose to run theirs as half-day camps, allowing teens who need to have jobs to work during the other part of the day.

Most camps are day camps, with campers going home at the end of the day. One camp, Corrupt the Youth, is a residential camp and focuses specifically on providing an "on-campus" experience for campers who might not ever imagine themselves going to college. Some camps receive full funding from their universities, while others depend on donors and grants, and still others are able to charge a fee while making accommodations for campers who are unable to afford those fees.

The second part of the book provides a select set of activities that have worked well for us. Not all camps contributed a separate activity, although several camps included a brief discussion of activities in their respective chapters. The contributions range from a lesson plan for an interactive philosophy of science activity to having a discussion of several themes in the *Harry Potter* books to a lesson plan to do with four-to-five-year-old children. We hope that, on the one hand, readers will find these helpful as they get started, but that, on the other, they will also not be afraid to develop their own activities, discussions, and themes to suit their campers and staff.

Finally, the third part of the book includes reflections by campers on their experiences at camp. We also included camper voices in the first philosophy camp volume. For this book, however, I specifically asked campers to discuss an activity, a reading, a method, and so on, that had an impact on them so that readers could hear from the campers themselves what worked and what did not work. My aim is for readers to see the variety of models, activities, approaches, methods, and themes that can be used to build a philosophy camp appropriate to the community in which one resides. The appendix comprises an excerpt from a longer meta-study on why pre-college philosophy programs succeed.

Whichever model you use to design your camp, we wish you happy camping!

NOTES

1. Philosophy for Children, sometimes known in its abbreviated form, P4C, is a particular program in pre-college philosophy. It is among the earliest of such programs, certainly among those organized through a university or institute, and is a model from which many others have developed. For more information on P4C, see the following: The Institute for the Advancement of Philosophy for Children. https://

www.montclair.edu/iapc/Accessed on line, November 30, 2019; A brief history of P4C https://p4c.com/about-p4c/history-of-p4c/; Michael Pritchard's entry on Philosophy for Children in the Stanford Encyclopedia of Philosophy. https://plato.stanford.edu/entries/children/ Accessed online November 30, 2019.

2. Douglas Martin, "Matthew Lipman, Philosopher and Educator," Dies at 87, *New York Times*, January 14, 2011. Accessed online, August 21, 2019. https://www.nytimes.com/2011/01/15/education/15lipman.html.

3. Pamela Matthews, "Philosophy for the Young, Curious, and Hungry," in Claire Elise Katz, ed. *Growing Up with Philosophy Camp* (Lanham, MD: Rowman & Littlefield, 2020).

4. For general information see: https://p4ctexas.sites.tamu.edu/. For camp contact information and other resources see, https://p4ctexas.sites.tamu.edu/2017/02/24/resources/.

Part I

HOW TO START, ORGANIZE, AND RUN A PHILOSOPHY CAMP

Chapter 1

Observations on the Aggie School of Athens

Running a Philosophy Summer Camp in South Central Texas

Claire Elise Katz

The Aggie School of Athens, the philosophy camp run by Texas A&M University, hosted its inaugural camp in June 2016.[1] The philosophy camp has run each summer in June since then, concluding its fifth summer in June 2020. This chapter provides the nuts and bolts of running this particular philosophy camp, from curriculum to demographics to funding, and many of the other logistics that help the camp run smoothly. Although some details are specific to running a camp on the Texas A&M campus (and in Texas), many have general applicability.

CURRICULUM

In 2016, the inaugural camp, we organized the week around themes that we thought would be of particular interest to precollege students while also providing a broad view of the discipline. We asked the following questions: What is philosophy? What does it mean to be ethical? What makes a society just or unjust? What is the ideal form of education? What is art? What does it mean to be human and how would you represent that in a time capsule?[2] Beginning each day with a reading from Plato, we engaged the campers in lively discussions about the history of these ideas and their continued importance for contemporary society. The campers connected Plato's questions from 2,500 years ago to difficult and often painful problems such as police brutality, gender socialization, surveillance, and socioeconomic inequality.

On the first day of camp we introduced Plato's Allegory of the Cave by showing the campers what we now refer to as the "creepy claymation" video.[3] We discussed the idea of epistemic chains, that is, the constraints on our beliefs that prevent us from seeing beyond what we already believe or think we know to be true. We then discussed Plato's contention that various epistemic chains, much of our everyday views, prevent most human beings from turning toward the truth. That afternoon the middle schoolers contemplated the nature of their own chains in a discussion of gender equality.

After viewing and discussing an episode of the PBS series, *Brain Games*, which covered stereotypes of male and female behavior (e.g., spatial relations and memory), many of the middle schoolers quickly asserted that there were not relevant differences between the sexes.[4] They also identified the problems in the testing scenario. For example, one camper stated that the sample size was too small from which to make any kind of generalization about one sex or the other. By "relevant" we meant that whatever differences do exist between the sexes they should not be viewed as having an effect on whether we would consider one sex to be smarter, or more generally, better at a particular skill than the other.

We have no doubt that our campers really held this view that there are not relevant differences. But how one sees differences and the effects of that might be more subtle than our campers were initially acknowledging. One counselor pushed them a bit and asked, "How is this classroom organized?" After a long pause and some glances around the room, the knowing smiles emerged. Both the boys and the girls were clustered throughout the room in clusters of boys and in clusters of girls.

"But we're just sitting with our friends," one camper replied, defending the segregated arrangement. "Can boys and girls be friends?," another camper asked. "What are we assuming by asking this question?," queried a counselor. "That friendships are not in-love relationships and that in-love relationships are only between males and females," replied yet another camper. "But that's not true," she continued. "People of the same sex can be in love.... So maybe gender differences—and our friendships—are more complicated than we normally like to admit," this same eleven-year-old girl observed. "Maybe *these* are our chains."

In a session with the high school students on what makes for a just society, a discussion of race ensued:

"Are natural kinds (groups that form naturally) 'real'?"
"How do natural kinds relate to race?"
"Do parents of different races have different expectations for their kids?"
"Aren't these stereotypes?"
"Do stereotypes have any truth to them?"

Our group of high school students raised these questions within a candid discussion about race and ethnicity. What could have been a volatile shouting match about race became the springboard for a thoughtful conversation about identity and about how to have difficult conversations.

A discussion of surveillance within the context of Jeremy Bentham's panopticon, a design which allows a single guard to observe all inmates within an institution, prompted one high school girl to vent about school dress codes: "[They] make me feel like I'm constantly being watched and controlled." Sharing her view with the group, she cleared a space for other young women to voice their concerns. Guided by the question, "What are schools explicitly and implicitly teaching?," the campers contributed their views to the larger conversation about how schools should (and do) operate.

THEMES FOR PHILOSOPHY CAMP IN SUCCESSIVE YEARS

2017: Philosophical Worlds: Chinese Philosophy, Philosophy of Religion, Philosophy of Science (figure 1.1).
2018: Democracy, Literacy, Education: Dewey, Freire, Federalist Papers (figure 1.2).
2019: *Harry Potter* and Philosophy: Censorship, Magic, Gender, Race and Identity (figure 1.3).

Each year we have had guest speakers or visitors. Two years in a row we had volunteers from the philosophy department. We also made use of Cushing, our special collections library. During the 2017 camp, Philosophical Worlds, the librarians made a display of literary maps (for example, *Harry Potter, Lord of the Rings*). The director of the Confucius Institute organized the entire day from facilitating discussion of Confucius and Daoism to lunch to the afternoon activities, which comprised a rotation of brush painting, Tai Chi, and calligraphy.

Figure 1.1 A Philosophical World Collage. *Source*: Claire Katz (Texas A&M).

Figure 1.2 Making Paper at the Cushing Library. *Source*: Texas A&M.

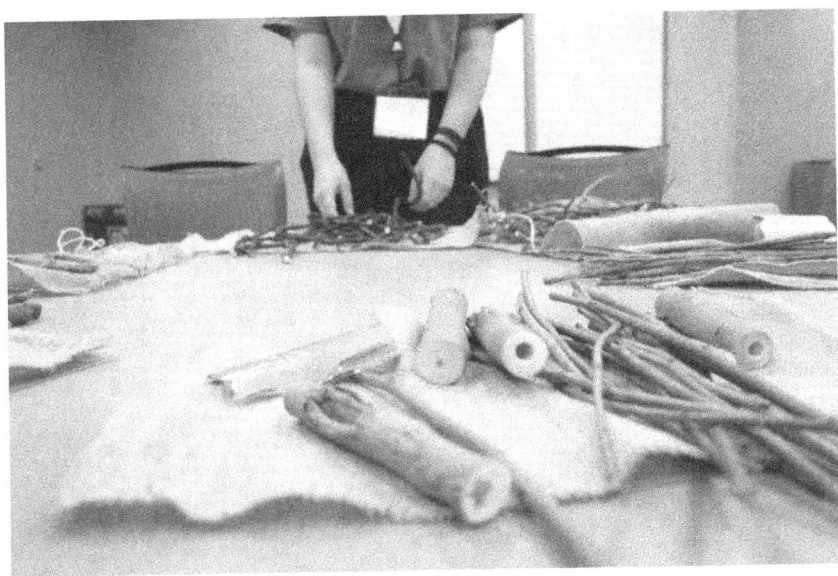

Figure 1.3 Making Wands. *Source*: Desirae Embree.

	Monday	Tuesday	Wednesday	Thursday	Friday
	Introduction & Cave Allegory	**Freedom, The Future, and Ethics**	**Mark Mitton--Magician**	**Identity, Family, and Hogwarts**	**Wandmaking, Party**
	Coffee:	Coffee:	Coffee:	Coffee:	Coffee:
8:30	Drop Off	Drop Off	Drop Off	Drop Off	Drop Off
9:00	Go to X	Go to X	Go to X	Go to X	Go to X
9:30	Intro & Rules HS: **Lead** MS: **Lead**	Foreknowledge & Freedom	Guest: Mark Mitton	Gender & Education	Wandlore and Wandmaking
10:00					
10:30	Snack	Snack	Snack	Snack	Snack
1:00	Cave Allegory				
11:30					
12:00	Lunch: Pizza (*X helps with lunch*)	Lunch: MSC	Lunch: Blue Baker	Lunch: MSC	Lunch: Pizza
12:30					
1:00	Censorship & Dangerous Knowledge Possible activity: What censored books have you read?	Family and Belonging?	Magic and Science--what's the difference?	HS: Race, Natural Kinds & Representation MS: Animals, Patroni	Skits & Certificates
1:30					
2:00					
2:30	Snack	Snack/Skit practice	Snack/Skit practice	Snack/Skit practice	Snack
3:00					
3:30	Pick up	Pick up	Pick up	Pick up	Pick up
4:00					
			Magic Show at 8pm Rudder Forum		

Figure 1.4 Sample Camp Schedule 2019. *Source*: Claire Katz (Texas A&M).

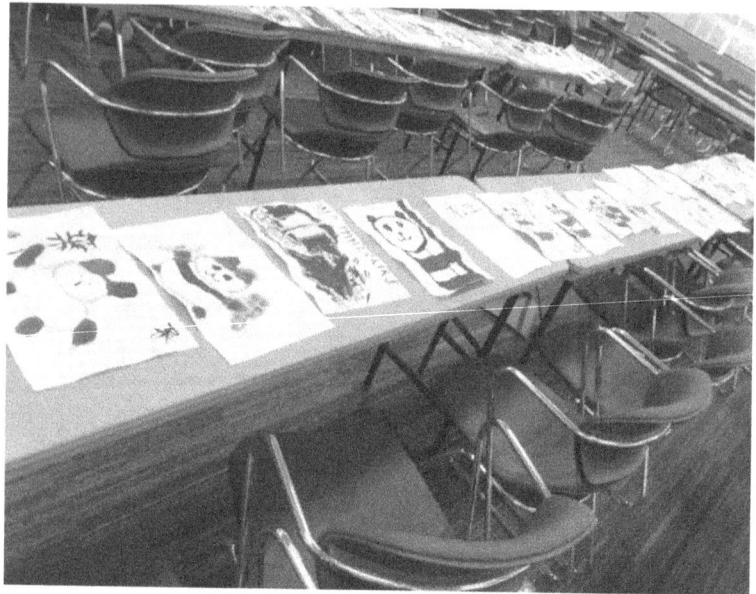

Figure 1.5   Brush Painting (2017). *Source*: Claire Katz (Texas A&M).

Figure 1.6   Mark Mitton, Magician (2019). *Source*: Claire Katz (Texas A&M).

The following year when we discussed literacy, the librarians helped the students make paper from pulp, print a Federalist paper from the printing press, and give a presentation on political pamphlets and zines. Our most recent camp hosted Mark Mitton, a magician from New York City and the Worthwich School of wand-making (figure 1.6).

SAMPLE READING LIST: DEMOCRACY, LITERACY, EDUCATION

Philosophy Camp 2018
Theme: Democracy, Literacy, and Education
Descartes, *Meditations*
Dewey, *Creative Democracy*
DuBois, *Does the Negro Need Separate Schools*
Hamilton, Federalist No 70
Madison, Federalist No 10
Douglass, *Narrative of the Life of Frederick Douglass* (excerpt)
Freire, *Pedagogy of the Oppressed*, chapters 2 and 3
hooks, excerpt from *Teaching to Transgress*
Plato, "Crito"
Plato, "Meno"
Plato, *Republic*, Book VII
Weil, *On the Abolition of Political Parties*, excerpt

PEDAGOGY

The day before our first day of the 2016 philosophy summer camp, the philosophy camp staff met for a follow-up pedagogy workshop. We had discussed pedagogy previously, but on this day, we did a more intensive training. Somewhere in the middle of the workshop, one of the staff—an assistant professor of philosophy and accomplished teacher—stopped, looked up, and then made a statement, as if the result of a light bulb having gone off: "We are not using notes, are we?" "No," I replied, "no notes." "Oh my," he said. And that pretty much sums up our approach to pedagogy during the camp week.

We loosely follow the Philosophy for Children (P4C) pedagogy. The two primary themes we take from P4C is the emphasis on the discussion being participant-centered and the development of a community of inquiry. Our aim is to engage the campers in close readings of short philosophical texts—sometimes just a paragraph—to help them figure out what a text says. We then move from the text to a discussion, allowing the discussion to move in a philosophical direction with the questions and responses from the campers being the drivers of that discussion.

RECRUITING STAFF

Philosophy students—both undergraduate and graduate students—make excellent teachers. With training in methodology that puts the campers at the center of the discussion, they make fantastic facilitators. I developed a senior-level course focused on teaching undergraduates, and graduate students if interested, to teach philosophy to children. This course produces several students each spring who are interested in volunteering with the camp. The course is offered in the spring semester and comprises both a seminar and lab component.

The seminar comprises readings in the history of philosophy from Plato, Rousseau, and Dewey; P4C pedagogy (Matthew Lipman and Ann-Margaret Sharp on P4C methodology and community of inquiry); philosophy of childhood (Gareth Matthews); and theoretical essays on teaching philosophy to young people—ethics, epistemology, metaphysics, existentialism, and so forth. The course uses the methodology in the class, with one exception: students do the reading before class, rather than in class as a community.

What I discovered each spring I teach the course is that the methodology works just as well on college students as it does with pre-college students and my college students are better philosophers at the end of the course. With the practical requirement—they must facilitate at least one philosophy discussion with pre-college students during the semester—they also discover not only that they are adept teachers but also that they like teaching. Closer in age to the campers, the college students are often better facilitators—for example, they have cultural references at their fingertips.

In some cases, I was able to compensate the undergraduates. Our students at A&M are unusual insofar as many come to this campus because of the selfless service ethos. Some students wish to have the experience teaching and others do this as part of service requirements for other organizations. The graduate students gain experience developing a course syllabus, learn an alternative pedagogy, and practice leading discussions. They also develop the knowledge and experience of doing philosophy outside of a college classroom, which they can take with them when they are (hopefully) gainfully employed.[5]

DEMOGRAPHICS

Some aspects of our demographics remain consistent. Each year, the camp enrollment evenly divides between campers who identify as male and campers who identify as female. Additionally, slightly more than one-third of the campers identified as nonwhite (this would include South Asian, Asian, nonwhite Hispanic, and African American) and/or as part of a minority belief system within the context of this community. This would include Muslim, Jewish, and non-Western (e.g., Hindu). With few exceptions, our campers are students in the public schools.[6]

Staff demographics have been relatively consistent over the four years we have offered the camp. For camps hosted in 2016–2019 the director has been a white woman, full professor in the Department of Philosophy. We have had three additional white male faculty members, all holding a PhD in philosophy. Graduate students on the staff comprise a diversity of backgrounds, including white, Hispanic, and Asian women, and Hispanic, white, and Black men.

Other than the regular graduate student staff, different graduate students participate each year based on interest and availability. There is an open application process, but we do require training and participation in the pedagogy workshops offered in the fall and the spring semesters. In 2017, we had two Latinx graduate students working on their PhDs in Hispanic Studies who offered a dual-language philosophy component to the camp. Graduate students also provided intellectual diversity: English, Africana Studies, Film Studies, Women's Studies, Philosophy, and Hispanic Studies. We typically have between nine and fourteen staff each year.

The undergraduate facilitators are frequently drawn from my P4C class, which is usually offered in the spring semester of the academic year. Undergraduates led philosophy discussions in small groups. The gender balance of the undergraduates varies.

CAMPER DEMOGRAPHICS AND CAMPER APPLICATION

In 2016, the camp enrolled a diverse forty-six students from sixty applications. The enrollments were evenly divided between middle school and high school (ages eleven to seventeen), with approximately equal numbers of those identifying as females and males in each age group. Roughly a third identified as nonwhite, with the rest as white/non-Hispanic. One half—regardless of ethnicity or gender—identified as academically inclined toward the STEM fields.

Although most of the campers were from the local community in Bryan-College Station, Texas, several campers enrolled from other cities in Texas (Dallas, Austin, Houston, and beyond), a few from outside Texas completely, and one from Paris, France.

The following summer in 2017, we enrolled 64 campers out of nearly 100 applications. Exactly half identified as either male or female (as identified by parents referring to their son/daughter) in each of the middle and high groups with roughly one-third who identified as nonwhite and roughly one-third who identified as non-Christian. A similar percentage to 2016 identified as interested in the STEM fields. As a sidenote, the 2017 camp was simply too large. Our youth advisory board's primary suggestion has been to keep the camp on the smaller side, and they are correct in this suggestion.

In both 2018 and 2019 we made significant efforts to reduce the size of the camp. In 2018 with more than 100 applicants, we accepted 58 campers. We used an application that asked specific questions not only for the campers to answer but also for their parents to answer. Given a couple of problems that we encountered in 2017 with parents not being completely sure about what philosophy camp entailed, we wanted to make sure that everyone was on the same page. We also eliminated the teacher recommendation since many of these would reference a gifted and talented program. We were interested in students who were intellectually engaged but in ways that traditional school cannot always identify.

In 2019 we reduced the camp back to the original number of forty-six campers. And in 2020, we reduced the camp to twenty-five campers. For both 2018 and 2019, the demographics are similar to previous years with at least half of the campers identifying as female. More than half of our middle school campers in 2018 were returning campers. For 2020, all twenty-five campers would be returning campers with approximately 75 percent having attended camp for at least three and in some cases all four previous summers.

A WORD ABOUT PHILOSOPHY AS A DISCIPLINE

The demographics for the Aggie School of Athens philosophy summer camp do not match the demographics of professional philosophy. Data gathered by Kate Norlock on women in academic philosophy in the United States revealed that, as of June 2011, "roughly, among full-time instructional faculty, women are 16.6% of the 13,000 total full-time philosophy faculty (that is, 2,158), and 26% of the 10,000 part-time instructors (that is, 2,600). In other words, women are 4,758 of the 23,000 or so: 20.69%."[7]

The numbers and percentages are significantly lower for philosophers who identify as nonwhite. Working with the camp, in which students identified either as oriented toward the STEM fields and/or as nonwhite or not male (and nearly every student fell into one category or the other, or both), we found a very different picture of philosophical community and dialogue. Our experience with the campers reminded us that philosophy is compelling across lines of gender and ethnicity (figure 1.7).

FUNDING

The Aggie School of Athens has been fortunate with regard to funding and we have been able to provide the camp at no charge for all camper families. The camp has enjoyed generous support from the Public Partnership and Outreach (PPO), Office of the Provost, and the College of Liberal Arts. Hosting the camp on a university campus, we are able to take advantage of many

Figure 1.7 High School (2016). *Source*: Texas A&M.

free or low-cost opportunities: classrooms are free and larger rooms (e.g., auditoria, theaters, etc.) are deeply discounted since our camp is hosted by an academic unit.

The first two summers, the camp received a substantial grant from the associate dean for Graduate Research and Professional Development in the College of Liberal Arts.[8] The grant provided funding to pay the stipends for the graduate students and most if not all of the supplies—T-shirts, course packs, insurance, background checks, snacks, and so forth. Generous funding from the PPO office enabled us to provide lunch for campers and staff during the camp week. The director was paid summer salary by the dean of the College of Liberal Arts.

For the next three years, funding was guaranteed through a Memorandum of Understanding among three units: PPO, College of Liberal Arts, and the Department of Philosophy. Additionally, in fall 2017, I was awarded the Murray and Celeste Fasken Chair in Distinguished Teaching, which provided funds to compensate the graduate students and the staff for summers 2018 and 2019.

In 2019, the camp tried a few ambitious activities. To support the theme of Harry Potter and philosophy, we arranged for two outside guests. Mark Mitton, a magician located in New York City, visited the camp and provided an exciting demonstration on the relationship between magic and knowledge. Additional funding for the academic part of Mark's visit was supported by the Glasscock Center for Humanities Research. Mark's evening magic show allowed us to ask for financial support from other groups who might benefit from his visit, for example, the Aggie Swim Camp, using Texas A&M's facilities, provided additional funding.

We also hosted the Worthwich Ladies who run a wand-making school in Austin, Texas. Our campers were able to fashion a wooden wand in a manner that fit their respective personalities. The Aggie School of Athens deeply appreciates the generous funding it has received, without which the camp could not have provided many of the experiences that allowed the campers to feel like they are part of a community (figure 1.8).

Figure 1.8 On Our Way to the Session on Philosophy, Epistemology, and Philosophy with Magician Mark Mitton (2019). *Source*: Claire Katz (Texas A&M).

Local businesses, especially those that provide our lunches, have been supportive. In exchange for a statement about the business on our website, a local pizza place gave us a considerably reduced rate for pizza, salads, and drinks; the sandwich place we used provided all the drinks and paper products at no charge. If a camp is okay with adding a sponsor to a T-shirt, it might find other support around their local community. The university admissions office might also be willing to provide some funding since it is in their interest to bring pre-college aged kids to campus for an academic program.

CAMPER ADVISORY BOARD

Beginning in fall 2018, the Aggie School of Athens developed a Camper Advisory Board, comprising about twenty campers of varying ages. The board provides feedback for the camp: camp size, themes, topics, activities, and so forth. Additionally, the board meets monthly on a weekend evening during the school year to watch and discuss a movie, usually with dinner. Engaging in philosophical discussions throughout the year allows those campers devoted to philosophy to continue developing their intellectual and social community.

CHALLENGES

For the most part, each philosophy camp has run successfully. Working with so many kids of varying ages and backgrounds, we will always experience some complaints—the lunches are not to everyone's taste, the themes are not always of interest to everyone, drop-off/pickup are complicated, too many forms, and so forth. The advisory board provided significant advice about the need to do a better job of integrating new campers (first-time campers) into the well-formed intellectual community. They also advised us to make the camp smaller in size. We did both of those things. The challenge for us is wanting to include more campers, but we recognize that the larger the camp, the more diminished the experience for everyone—thus no one benefits by being admitted to a philosophy camp that is simply too large for engaged discussions.

There is a tension between "doing" activities and engaging in philosophical discussion. Striking the right balance is not always an easy task. During the year when we discussed philosophy of religion, we had a camper who complained that we were running an "anti-God" camp. The accusation surprised us since the person who led that session is a philosophy professor who adheres to the Christian faith. The challenge then for all philosophy camps is ensuring that parents and campers understand—to some degree—what philosophy is before they attend camp. Philosophy questions can appear threatening. Not everyone is prepared for that. After running the camp for five summers, we now believe we have ironed out most of the kinks—though we are sure, having said this, new ones will emerge.

Our challenge has been to attract/recruit more students from socioeconomically challenged backgrounds. We are not unaware of the many reasons for this challenge, not the least of which would be demands on the time for teens from this background. To recruit youth from this demographic not only do we need to be prepared for the camp to be free of charge, which it already is, but also we need to be able to provide transportation (Bryan/College Station does not have adequate public transportation) and a stipend to compensate for time that could be used to earn wages.

GENERAL LESSONS WE HAVE LEARNED

- Smaller is better—if you can go with fewer campers, that will make for a more enjoyable camp experience (or by smaller, dividing up the campers into smaller discussion group).
- Develop a camp application that allows you to identify campers who are a good fit for your camp. These prospective campers are not necessarily the students who score the highest on tests or have the highest grades. They are often the students who feel the most disengaged from school. Include a question on the application for parents, for example, "Why do you want your child to come to philosophy camp?" or "What do you hope your child gets out of attending philosophy camp?" Answering, "helping to get X into college" is probably a red flag.
- Have campers develop camp rules for discussions/behaving at camp and stick to them. Campers know exactly what is needed for this—they come to camp to have these discussions and they are frustrated by the campers who are not there for that purpose. Campers notice those who are always on their phones texting, and so on. Our "no-phone" rule was suggested by our campers and it worked incredibly well.

- Activities on the first day can set the tone for the week and are often referred to through the week. We have done several activities that have worked really well.
  - The Claymation video of Plato's Allegory of the Cave: We have used this on the first day of camp every year. It works great especially because the campers see things in subsequent viewings and discussions that they did not see previously, signaling to them their own growth. It also works to pair it with the text from Plato's *Republic*. Our campers refer to the themes in the allegory throughout the week.[9]
  - Philosophical speed dating: Develop a set of questions that will be used throughout the week. Set up the campers in two rows facing each other. Set the time for ninety seconds to two minutes. They need to introduce themselves to each other and discuss the question. When the timer goes off, campers move to their left. They are now facing a new person, with a new question. This gives them an opportunity to discuss the questions that will be approached during the week and to consider what they think about these themes before they hear what others think. I have also used this activity in my college classes.
  - The Hobbes Game.[10] We did this game with the high school students on the first afternoon of the first camp in 2016. None of the high school students knew each other before camp started. It was a great way to teach social contract theory, and like the cave allegory, because of the themes we were discussing that week in political philosophy, the campers referred to the game throughout the week.
- Use campers' ideas as much as possible—the campers who return are committed to the camp and their thoughtful ideas have been helpful for making our camp better each year. In 2019, we used Harry Potter for the theme, which was suggested to us by a camper.
- Include campers in the development of the curriculum—What are they interested in?
- Avoid cramming the curriculum—one theme per day and spending more time on individual readings allows the campers to explore the ideas in depth and develop sustained conversations.
- Figure out for the individual camp the right length of time for a break—enough to visit and continue conversations, but not so long they get bored.
- Encourage campers to continue philosophy discussions outside of camp. One of our philosophy campers started a philosophy club at her high school. The core of the club includes about six of our veteran philosophy campers. Through the club, they will have an impact on their peers at

school and continue making connections between their philosophical connections and the world around them. One of our philosophy undergraduate minors, a former camper and a current facilitator, is facilitating the discussions with them.
- T-shirts are not only a fun way to give identity to your camp but also a safety feature for identifying campers and staff (see figure 1.9a and figure 1.9b). We were advised to do the shirts in two different colors—one for campers and one for staff so that each group could be easily identified.

The last afternoon of camp we have a celebration where we distribute certificates, the campers display their creative projects or perform skits, we have pizza and cake, the latter designed and baked by Dee Dee Leverett, a staff person in the Public Partnership Office (figure 1.10a and figure 1.10b).

At the end of that first camp in 2016, one camper confided that the most amazing thing about philosophy camp was the experience of believing one thing in the morning when she arrived and by the end of the day believing something else because her views had been gently challenged and the facts she had believed in were shown to be incorrect. Her confession revealed to us the extraordinary honesty and integrity with which the young people approached the camp. It also revealed the intellectual courage they demonstrate through the week. We have found that over the years, the more we allow the campers to participate in the development of the camp, the more the camp really is their camp about which they care deeply.

Every summer we end our camp by staging a reproduction of Raphael's School of Athens on the steps of the building that houses the philosophy department. We are fortunate that the building has beautiful columns, projecting the image of a location in ancient Greece. Our image is updated with gender and racial diversity, and of course the books everyone is holding. Figure 1.11 shows the picture from 2019, run through the Waterlogue app both for effect and to protect the identities of the campers.

PHILOSOPHY CAMP IN THE SUMMER OF THE PANDEMIC

A brief note about philosophy camp in 2020: I am adding a few remarks here to indicate what we did when our face-to-face version of the camp

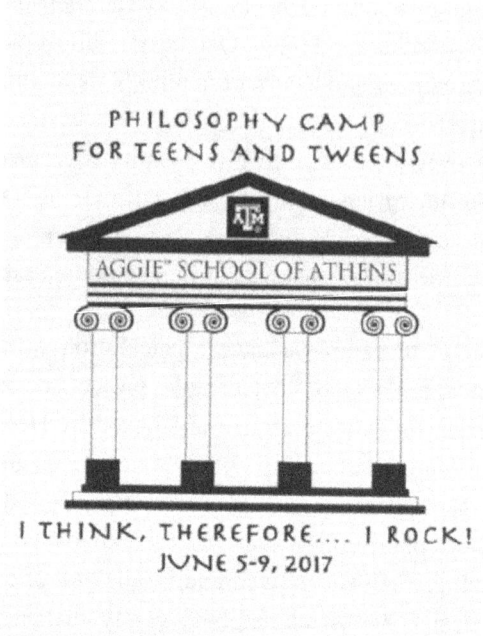

Figures 1.9a and 1.9b Images from the 2017 Camp T-Shirts (Front and Back) Are Not Only Fun But Also for Safety So that Campers Can Be Identified. *Source*: Claire Katz (Texas A&M).

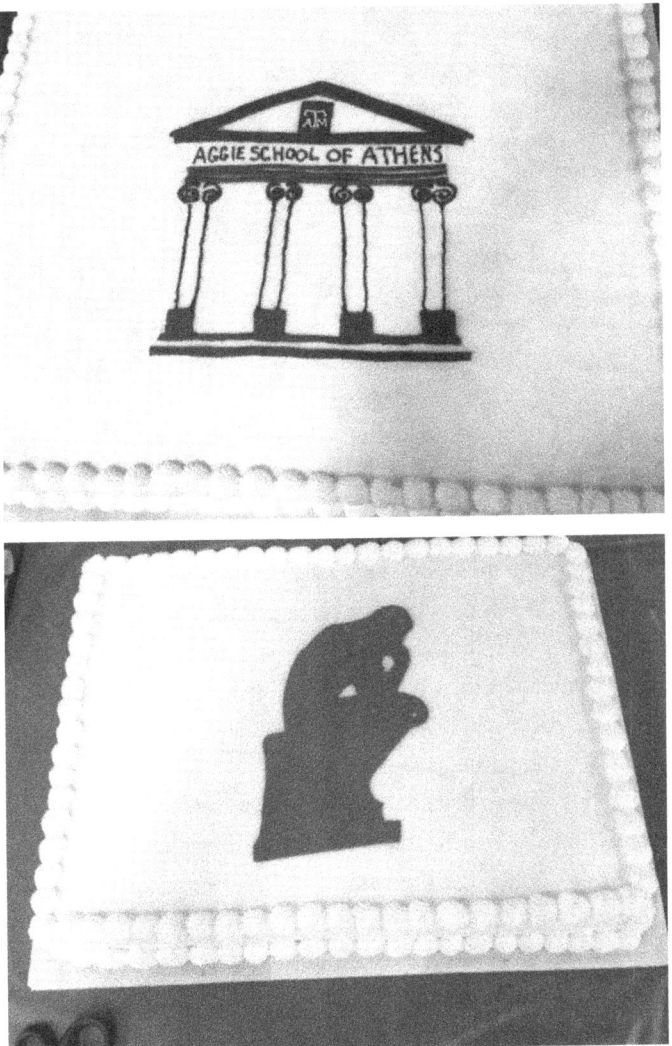

Figures 1.10a and 1.10b Cake with the Aggie School of Athens Logos, Designed and Baked by Dee Dee Leverett. *Source*: Claire Katz (Texas A&M).

was canceled. I know that many camps made a choice to cancel their camps altogether. We chose to move our camp online. During the spring semester when the K–12 schools moved to remote learning, we started offering weekly discussions about themes related to the pandemic, including a discussion of Camus's *The Plague* and Foucault's *Discipline and Punish*. Not all of our philosophy campers participated in those discussions, but enough did so we were able to get a sense of how camp discussions might work.

Figure 1.11 Staging Raphael's School of Athens on the Steps of the YMCA Building, Texas A&M. *Source*: Claire Katz (Texas A&M).

Additionally, several of the philosophy camp parents were also interested in these discussions/themes. Since the first summer we started the philosophy camp, parents would ask us when we were going to have a philosophy camp for parents. Moving to remote learning allowed us to do that, especially since some of our camper families lived in cities at least two to three hours from College Station. As a result, we added a second weekly discussion of the same material for the parents.

Thinking about how to organize the camp, we set aside our original theme, readings, activities, and so forth. We picked a few themes that the campers had suggested. We extended the camp for three weeks. We met MWF from 2:00 p.m. to 4:00 p.m. in the afternoon. We used the third week to discuss topics that the campers generated. We did not require any reading in advance of the afternoon discussions and all discussions were conducted synchronously.

The online version was by no means ideal, but we felt that offering some version of a camp was better than not offering anything. For us, offering an online version allowed us to keep the campers who were interested engaged in philosophy and engaged with each other. In some ways, the extended time worked really well, giving campers a chance to think about themes and discussions over a longer period of time. The face-to-face element was sorely missed as were all of the social dimensions of camp: lingering in a hallway, having lunch together, and just the physical presence of each other mattered.

NOTES

1. For more information on our program and to contact us: https://p4ctexas.sites.tamu.edu/. In November 2020, we were notified that P4C Texas/Aggie School of Athens Philosophy Summer Camp for Teens is the recipient of the 2020 APA/PDC Prize for Excellence and Innovation in Philosophy Programs.

2. For more on the individual discussions, see the essay by Katz and Embree in *Growing Up with Philosophy Camp: How Thinking Develops Friendship, Community, and a Sense of Self* (Lanham, MD: Rowman & Littlefield, 2020).

3. See, http://platosallegory.com/. We show this video every summer on the first morning of camp. See Evelyn Conway, "Leaving the Cave," in *Growing Up with Philosophy Camp* op. cit.

4. The *Brain Games* episode set up the differences in terms of a binary. The middle school campers followed this structure. By contrast, the high school students discussed gender and sexuality with the recognition that gender and sexuality are multiple.

5. I am happy to share my course syllabus and experiences teaching this class.

6. Our aim each summer has been to increase the diversity of the camp participants, especially with regard to socioeconomics. However, our area lacks good public transportation and many of the high school age kids work. Our hope is to secure a grant that would allow us to compensate campers for time off from work and also provide transportation to and from camp.

7. See Kate Norlock, APA Committee on the Status of Women, published in 2006; updated 2011 https://docs.google.com/viewer?a=v&pid=sites&srcid=ZGVmYXVsdGRvbWFpbnxhcGFjb21taXR0ZWV2vbnRoZXN0YXR1c29md29tZW58Z3g6NTlmYTExZDBiY2U1MDliYw and https://docs.google.com/viewer?a=v&pid=sites&srcid=ZGVmYXVsdGRvbWFpbnxhcGFjb21taXR0ZWV2vbnRoZXN0YXR1c29md29tZW58Z3g6NGQxNWNhYWIzNmExOWNhZg. For more information, see http://www.apaonlinecsw.org/data-on-women-in-philosophy.

8. Our funding from the CASA grant was contingent on showing a work product to demonstrate the success of the camp. In 2017, I designed a longitudinal study with IRB approval. In 2019, I partnered with Rebecca Schlegel, a professor of social psychology, who helped design a set of survey questions that would measure changes in intellectual humility and authenticity. Even with a small sample size, preliminary results show an increase in intellectual humility and tolerance for others' views.

9. https://www.youtube.com/watch?v=69F7GhASOdM

10. This can be found in *Teaching Philosophy* 18(3):257–268·January 1995.

Chapter 2

Developing a Philosophy Summer Camp at the University of Kentucky

Caroline Buchanan, James William Lincoln, Suraj Chaudhary, Clay Graham, Andrew Van't Land, Lauren K. O'Dell, and Colin Smith

In the summer of 2015, a philosophy graduate student at the University of Kentucky (UK) organized the first annual UK Philosophy Camp. As the camp approaches its fifth season, its mission is clear: to help teens to grow intellectually and emotionally by developing their critical thinking skills and cultivating a passion for moral and civic engagement.[1] Adolescents are naturally eager to test the dogmas of their upbringing, and those who sign up for philosophy camp are looking for a constructive outlet to do so. Each annual camp has demonstrated that Kentucky youth need more opportunities to voice vital thoughts within a philosophical space.

In late April 2015, a handful of UK philosophy graduate students (led by Caroline Buchanan) assembled the inaugural camp. Their department was supportive financially, offering generous initial funding to get the program off the ground. Concerns about attracting enough students to the camp proved unfounded, as the counselors reached their planned cap of thirty students by relying on cold-e-mails to area high schools and word-of-mouth among supportive professors with adolescent children.

Many of the decisions made during the camp's first year set lasting precedents for the program. UK philosophy graduate students continue to organize and lead the (primarily high school age) camp free of charge. However, the camp's subsequent years have also offered new challenges and opportunities for improvement, most of which are connected to funding and curriculum development.

FUNDING

Following the first year of the camp, departmental funding became unavailable due to circumstances beyond the control of faculty and graduate students. Access to recurring institutional funding for the camp continues to be hampered by university budget priorities. In light of these constraints, departmental faculty have encouraged the graduate student counselors to implement an admission fee (a common practice for other local camps).

Yet the counselors have persistently rejected this advice, insisting that philosophy's ability to serve as a public good is contingent on its accessibility to individuals as a personal good.[2] They did not, and still do not, want to enable socioeconomic status as a gatekeeper to philosophical practice. Instead of charging the campers, they have chosen to take their program in a more philanthropic direction. They believe the camp has taken on a philanthropic identity because it pursues a vision of the public good, one in which philosophical practice is praised as part of the public space.[3]

In the camp's earlier years, this commitment to the idea that philosophy can serve the public good allowed the camp counselors to seek out and receive funding grants from agencies such as the Philosophy Learning and Teaching Organization (PLATO) and the American Philosophical Association's (APA) Berry Fund for Public Philosophy.[4] In later years, their funding would be secured through grants from organizations like the Society of Philosophers in America (SOPHIA) and from private donations by individuals who value publicly engaged and accessible philosophical practice beyond the traditional academy setting.[5]

Two primary issues have challenged the camp organizers in meeting philanthropic goals and fundraising needs. First, individual donations from faculty, staff, and the campers' parents are often difficult to renew on a yearly basis. Campers age out of the program, and subsequently their parents are less likely to donate to the camp. Second, most of the available grant programs (like those through PLATO and the APA) seem to operate on a seed-grant funding model rather than a sustained, renewable funding model. Seed-grant models are designed to provide a one-time infusion of funding to get programs started, but they do not provide funding beyond start-up.

Even though the camp's funding needs are rather minimal, the prevalence of the seed-grant funding model means that programs such as the UK Philosophy Camp can quickly exhaust the most obvious funding sources. The counselors have developed several tactics to increase the likelihood of securing funding:

I. *Track the Impact of the Program.* This can be done by implementing camper feedback surveys and a modest amount of photo-documentation. The successful use of seed-grant programs has enabled the UK Philosophy Camp to establish philanthropic credibility. Proper documentation of demonstrable impact is vital to motivate donors to continue giving.[6]

II. *Establish or Utilize a Tax-Deductible Fund.* This can be done through existing or new funds in the department or the school's philanthropy office. Such accounting is vital for securing a systems infrastructure for future grants and (ambitiously) a successful annual giving or capital campaign program. Fund accounts also provide donors with tax deduction documentation and with secure access to any free online giving platforms maintained by a school's philanthropy office.

III. *Utilize Free Online Giving Platforms.* It is advisable to avoid certain donation platforms, such as GoFundMe.com, which take a percentage of the total raised as a fee. However, it is helpful to use other platforms such as NetworkForGood.org in order to organize crowdfunding campaigns.[7] Such a platform, which enables peer fundraising initiatives and relationship building, can alleviate some of the organizing burden associated with fundraising.

IV. *Establish Community Partnerships.* This can be done to reduce costs and to spread information about the program. For instance, the UK Philosophy Camp has enjoyed an informal partnership with the UK Gaines Center for the Humanities, which has often offered free event space for the camp. Such partnerships can even lead to sponsorships that might be renewed on a recurring basis.

V. *Articulate a Philanthropic Vision.* Philanthropy has "for its end social progress, the continual development and self-realization of society."[8] The camp program at UK creates opportunities for philosophical practice as a personal good, which allows campers to engage in philosophy as a public good. By offering a free program, camp leadership facilitates the realization of a philanthropic vision: that philosophy is *for anyone*, can be practiced on some level *by anyone*, and that philosophical contributions to society can come *from anyone*. Articulating such a philanthropic vision gives donors reasons to give.

ACTIVITY STRUCTURE

In planning the camp's activities, counselors seek to balance academic rigor with fun. They strive to foster a sense of community by challenging each student to reflect and contribute. This typically involves mixing short readings and group discussions with games that yield philosophical upshots, hopefully ones related to topics they discuss. The counselors employ a plurality of activities and teaching methods, and the camp's multi-instructor format beneficially foregrounds the various strengths and interests of each instructor at different times.

Each seven-hour day features a morning session (9:00 a.m.–12:00 p.m.) and an afternoon session (1:00 p.m.–4:00 p.m.) split up by a lunch hour. Each session is planned and led by one of the counselors, each of whom is typically responsible for two such sessions throughout the week. During each session, the other instructors assist the primary instructor in facilitating discussions.

Each morning upon arrival, the campers engage with various warm-up activities such as logical puzzles and thought experiments. These exercises, which do not usually correlate with the days' themes, set the intellectual tone for the day without immediately inundating the camper with content. The campers enjoy this chance to get acquainted, work together, and exercise their minds in preparation for the day.

This is followed by either a group game or a short lecture and reading discussion. The latter sessions typically include an interactive lecture on a topic, a short reading, small group discussions among about four to six students and one instructor, and then a regrouping for a discussion among all campers and counselors. The counselors employ other teaching methods, such as think-pair-share exercises and worksheets, both for variety in activities and to meet the diverse range of learning styles.

The afternoon session after lunch begins with either a game or a lecture and discussion. It concludes with a journaling period in which students write responses to prompts regarding a theme, question, or problem that has arisen in the course of the day's activities. The final afternoon session of each camp typically has been a series of short presentations in which each student shares an entry from their week's journal entries and then discusses the subject with the entire group.

Perhaps the dyadic structure of lectures and games is intuitive and unsurprising. Yet each year, the counselors are surprised by which activities happen to succeed and which happen to fail. In one memorable example, a dense Aldo Leopold article on environmental philosophy sustained a surprising amount of student interest and discussion over the entire week, while Bertrand Russell's classic essay, "What Is Philosophy?," a perennial favorite, fell flat on its face. In this instance, the campers happened to be far more concerned about applied issues than theoretical subjects, and the counselors accordingly scrapped a few planned lectures on theoretical subjects for case studies.

Thus, as counselors implement their planned activities, it is important for them to remain attentive to the needs and interests of their immediate group of campers, and for them to be open to revising their schedule accordingly. For this and other reasons, the counselors have found that it is crucial for all instructors to be present for each session, and to be in constant dialogue about curricular alterations throughout the week.

Curriculum

Since its 2015 inception, the specific curriculum of the UK Philosophy Camp has changed considerably, even as its structure has remained fairly consistent. In its earliest iterations, the camp provided a general overview of key philosophical problems and ideas. Since then, however, the counselors have increasingly unified the philosophical content under a specific theme, for instance, the concept of justice (which was the camp theme in both 2017 and 2018). These opposite approaches—generalist versus thematic—have their own benefits and drawbacks, reflecting the inevitable trade-off between intellectual breadth and depth.

Yet even as the counselors have adjusted this ratio, they remain dedicated to the ultimate goal of providing campers with the material to explore philosophical ideas in an enjoyable, enlightening, and community-building manner. The camp's more recent thematic focus on justice has offered campers the opportunity to express, challenge, and enrich their own opinions about social issues. Camp sessions have covered topics such as property relations, intersubjectivity, environmental problems, social contracts, school funding, immigration, animal welfare, and much more.

In 2018, one of the most successful activities involved a discussion of racial justice, protest, and the NFL. A big reason for the success of this session is due to the involvement of SOPHIA. Members from this nonprofit's local chapter joined the campers for a mutually beneficial, cross-generational discussion of civil disobedience. Campers, counselors, and guests alike found this applied philosophy event to be lively and enlightening. One camper noted the "different point of view" he learned from SOPHIA members and that he was sympathetic to views he didn't expect to be.

Yet even successful sessions such as this SOPHIA forum manifest a persistent problem for the camp counselors: the near-uniformity of the camper's (progressive) political values. Because such ideological hegemony can prevent open and honest inquiry, the counselors have found it necessary to firmly guide the discussion so that the campers' views are challenged by piercing, directed questioning. Otherwise, the conversation can quickly devolve into a political echo chamber.

These challenges indicate that a camp's curriculum should not only reflect urgent and relevant subject material but also be designed in such a way that the philosophical heart of the subject surfaces naturally in dialogue and reflection. Therefore, it is highly valuable to have the counselors provide a structured mediating presence, both to guide campers in the right discursive direction and to give them the freedom to reach conclusions on their own.

The intellectual content of any structured philosophical inquiry (whether in a class, a reading group, or a summer camp) must always approach the participants on their own terms. This means that the exposures to ideas from the history of philosophy are not presented merely for the sake of textual analysis and understanding; instead, they are intended to aid in the camper's reflective self-development.

Camp counselors have found it invaluable to give campers an early opportunity to voice their interests and concerns, so the counselors may make adjustments based on the curiosities of that unique group. It may be of value to provide a quick survey or questionnaire during the camper application process in order to gauge what sort of curriculum will be most appropriate. One of the best ways to ensure that the camp will be a worthwhile experience for all participants is to tailor the curriculum to the needs or interests of the campers.

Student Campers

Throughout the camp's short history, the counselors have been encouraged both by successive waves of new campers and by the retention of certain campers from year to year. The counselors strive to expose the student campers to the lighthearted side of higher education years before the latter can even apply for college, thereby bridging the life-stage gap between the already stressful years of high school and the even more serious years of postsecondary education. The campers' ages range from thirteen to seventeen, with an average age of just over fifteen years old. On a few occasions, students yet to begin high school, but who are particularly interested in the opportunity, were also able to attend the camp.

Despite the sexism plaguing philosophy as a discipline (such as the underrepresentation of women), the UK Philosophy Camp attracts more females than males: nine (out of sixteen total) in 2017 and seven (out of ten total) in 2018. On the occasion that a student espouses resentful, aggressive, or dominating personalities, difficulties can manifest in sexist ways. Females and LQBTQ+ individuals can feel marginalized in conversation, and the historically combative stance of philosophical conversation can lead to male campers feeling more comfortable or even empowered to speak aggressively. This can lead to conversation "devolving" or being overpowered by a select few individuals.

In addition to sensitive dynamics among campers, student feedback affirms that "heavy" or sensitive content can marginalize some and discourage full group participation. One particular student discussion about sexual assault went on in a casual way among campers, but this casual discussion was, in some students' opinions, flippant. One of the campers was visibly upset before a counselor redirected the conversation.

This is an example of the ongoing struggle to make all of the campers feel welcome in contributing to emotionally and ideologically fraught discussions, particularly concerning ethics and social and political philosophy. Mediating a discussion of sensitive, controversial issues with anyone, but particularly minors, requires a level of pedagogical nuance, and counselors must judge carefully their level of preparedness to do so before choosing to proceed.

One of the missions of the camp has been to offer a portal into academic life not only to those privileged students already on the college track (including some children of university faculty) but also to under-resourced students, especially those from historically marginalized or disenfranchised populations. Despite the ubiquity of philosophy as a human activity, its disciplinary form is often unfamiliar to many people; this is especially so for marginalized students whose high schools have been starved of funding for the arts and humanities.

One memorable young camper expressed gratitude for having the space to ask questions she had been wanting to talk about but didn't know how. She explained that she has been writing and thinking about "philosophical" topics without even realizing it. She returned to our camp the next year. Parents, too, have e-mailed us words of appreciation: one mother noted that her child had been asking "big questions" that she didn't know how to answer, and that when she saw our camp advertised, she knew it would be right up her child's alley.

Unfortunately, at best, our camp's ethnic demographics have included only 25 percent nonwhite participants (who self-identified as African American, Asian, and Latinx). Socioeconomically, hunger and poor nutrition is an annual problem each summer break for Kentucky students on school lunch assistance programs, and the counselors suspect that some of their campers are members of that population (e.g., one camper specifically mentioned that other non-free camps were cost-prohibitive for her family and that having access to food at the camp made the week truly "life altering").[9]

With more funding, the counselors could provide campers with free shuttle transit (directly to and from their homes) and free breakfasts and lunches.[10] Such resources would open up the camp to a range of (especially black and Latinx) students whose financial barriers prevent them from attending even if they are personally interested and academically prepared.

Students have tended to rate their overall camp experience at least a nine on a ten-point scale, probably because of the relational interaction fostered by the small group environment. The counselors have attempted to create a relationship- and community-building environment. Activities like the group logic puzzles, the group sharing of personal reflections, and the hour-long picnic lunches help to build relationships and community, especially among those individuals who might tend to be more introverted or feel isolated. As one student reflected, "Even during breaks and lunch we discussed philosophy, so everyone was invested in the camp."

According to their feedback, the campers have also developed relationships that continue beyond the camp. Several in particular have maintained long-distance friendships during the school year and they plan to meet again during the next summer camp.

GRADUATE STUDENT COUNSELORS

Organizing and conducting the camps has been valuable for the graduate students in several ways. The camp provides a much-needed venue for engagement with the local community, something conspicuously lacking in philosophical education in general. This kind of interaction has often forced graduate students to translate their jargon-heavy ideas into everyday language. Such flexibility is necessitated not only by the need to make abstract concepts intelligible to a teenage population but also by the need to engage them with philosophy in the first place.[11]

The counselors' work at the camp, therefore, has served as a reminder to make philosophy relevant and accessible to those not already immersed in it, including the nonmajors in the philosophy classes they teach regularly. The camp has also offered the counselors opportunities to learn from each other. By attending one another's sessions, the counselors have avoided mistakes, built on successes, and given feedback to each other at the end of each day. Such an exchange of skills has also occurred in the context of organizing the camp, with camp counselors becoming camp directors in subsequent years and drawing on the expertise of previous directors.

Moreover, detailed reports written at the end of each camp provide future directors with a rough guideline for fundraising, content organization, and camp logistics. These reports also include valuable anonymized feedback from the campers, which help the counselors improve their curriculum and pedagogical techniques for the next year. As a program that requires detailed planning beyond the confines of traditional academia, the camp provides graduate students with a rare opportunity to develop skills (marketable in and beyond academia) that are traditionally ignored within philosophy departments.

Apart from offering pedagogical and professional benefits, the camp has also been a source of a small but welcome stipend for those involved (typically $300 for counselors and $500 for directors). This helps the graduate students pay their bills during the lean summer months until their TA stipends resume in the fall semester. Yet funding difficulties have occasionally led to camp counselors and directors volunteering to work without the promise of financial benefits.

The lack of regular summer income for philosophy graduate students often forces those who are U.S. citizens to take other jobs that are less relevant to their professional development and it forces international students without work visas to subsist on their often meager savings. Viewing the camp as one of the professionally enriching ways to support graduate students during summer, combined with the camp's potential for community outreach and departmental advertising, should encourage philosophy departments to continually invest in an annual summer camp employing graduate students.

CONCLUSION

The UK Philosophy Camp has been a positive opportunity for graduate students to develop new pedagogical skills working with a younger demographic with whom college instructors rarely interact. Moreover, this camp has functioned as a meaningful introduction into philosophy and critical thinking for younger students who would otherwise not be exposed to this type of thinking, and who might become interested in pursuing a philosophy major upon entering college. At a time when fewer students across the country are studying philosophy, such initiatives may be crucial to stabilizing a given department's pool of majors and minors.

Through detailed analysis of past years and careful planning of future camps, counselors believe the UK Philosophy Camp can achieve the goals that their summer camp was designed to accomplish. They also hope that it can act as a model for other developing programs, as they all find creative solutions to new problems in a changing educational ecosystem. By creatively exposing individuals at younger ages and in new communities to philosophy, the camp counselors hope to instill a long-lasting and far-reaching appreciation for the humanities as a whole.

NOTES

1. These needs have grown more potent under the austerity conditions, recently intensified by the Kentucky state government, which threaten civic institutions such as public education.
2. Christelle, A., Hay, S., Lincoln, J., & Weber, E. (Forthcoming). "Foundations for Communities of Philosophical Conversation," *Public Philosophy Journal*. Retrieved from: http://tinyurl.com/y5x67aun.
3. Payton, R., & Moody, M. (2008). *Understanding Philanthropy: Its Meaning and Mission*. Indianapolis, IN: Indiana University Press.
4. Where PLATO aims to fund programs making philosophy accessible to pre-college students, the Berry Fund aims to support programs that create opportunities to demonstrate the personal value and social value of philosophy. See https://www.plato-philosophy.org/ and https://www.apaonline.org/page/grants.
5. See also SOPHIA: https://www.philosophersinamerica.com/?s=seed&submit=Search.
6. Salamon, L.M. (1992). *America's Nonprofit Sector: A Primer*. New York: Foundation Center.
7. There are many guides about how to engage in crowdfunding campaigns online. London South Bank University's "A Guide to Running Your Crowdfunding Campaign" offers helpful instructions for new practitioners. Causvox's "Ultimate Guide to Peer-to-Peer Fundraising" is a good resource for determining if peer-to-peer campaigns will benefit the program. The University of Kentucky's Center for Student Philanthropy's "Resource Guide for Corporations and Foundations" is a useful primer on institutional partnerships.
8. Huntington, J. O. S. (1892). "Philanthropy and Morality," *International Journal of Ethics* 3(1), p. 40–41.
9. Kentucky is one of the lowest performers for Summer Nutrition Support Programs for Kids <http://www.frac.org/wp-content/uploads/2017-summer-nutrition-report-1.pdf>. Food insecurity exists in every county in Kentucky <https://www.kyagr.com/Kentucky-AGNEWS/2016/Hunger-study-finds-food-insecurity-levels-remain-historically-high.html>.
10. This is also a recommendation in the Summer Nutrition Report above, which makes special note to call out Kentucky and highlights transportation assistance: "Kentucky—a very rural state—continues to see growth in various mobile summer meal initiatives, ranging from retrofitted school buses to library bookmobiles. Making the meals 'mobile' allows sponsors to more easily connect with children in underserved, hard-to-reach communities—especially in rural areas."
11. Despite the fact that the camp tends to attract students already interested in philosophical questions, their perceptions of the discipline often do not align with what they find in the camp.

Chapter 3

The Iowa Lyceum

Landon D. C. Elkind and Gregory Stoutenburg

INTRODUCING THE IOWA LYCEUM

The Iowa Lyceum first ran in June 2013. Iowa Lyceum founders Gregory Stoutenburg and Kristopher Phillips[1] read a news article about a precollege program at the University of Illinois and decided to start a philosophy camp at University of Iowa, where they were both graduate students in philosophy. Neither had experience with philosophy outreach, but were excited by the prospect of bringing philosophy to a population that has little access to it—public school students in the United States.

The goal of the program, then as now, was to introduce interested students to philosophy and critical thinking as useful skills and as a crucial part of a life lived well. The program still operates much as it did in its inaugural year, which as of this writing makes the program seven years old.

ORGANIZATIONAL POSITIONS

The Lyceum has two basic organizational positions. The first is the president, which is currently occupied by three graduate students who serve as copresidents. All administrative responsibilities fall to the president role. These tasks include scheduling rooms for Lyceum sessions, putting out advertisements for students, recruiting faculty and other graduate students to present at the Lyceum, ordering food, serving as the main contact for student participants and their parents, and so on. Some of the tasks can or must be delegated, such as room scheduling, which is done by the department's administrative assistant, but the rest is up to the copresidents.

The copresident structure was adopted very early in the Lyceum's history to ensure a smooth succession of leadership. Since graduate students in philosophy at the University of Iowa typically take about five years to complete their PhD, a copresident leadership typically comprises one senior graduate student and one junior graduate student. This ensures that by the time the junior student becomes the senior one, that person will have served as copresident for a few years, all the while learning the recent administrative history of the program from the senior president.

When the senior president leaves the role, the two copresidents together choose a new junior student as new copresident. The new student asked to serve as copresident is someone who has shown interest in the program and excellence as a teaching assistant in their graduate teaching responsibilities.

The second main role is that of volunteer or instructor. In a way, everyone who helps execute the Lyceum is a volunteer, because no one is paid for work associated with the Lyceum: we use the volunteer label more specifically to mean those volunteers who are serving the Lyceum, but not in an administrative capacity. Lyceum volunteer instructors lead the overwhelming majority of individual content sessions, described below.

There are several volunteer instructors for each Lyceum week. Volunteers typically teach one or two sessions depending on need and interest, with senior faculty members being the most likely to teach multiple sessions. One reason volunteers are happy to lead a session for the Lyceum is that we make it easy to do so: it is exciting and not very difficult to put together a sub-one-hour session on a topic of one's own interest, and to teach it to a group of students who are excited to be there. By relying on an array of volunteers, the Lyceum is able to present a diverse set of philosophical interests to participants.

LOGISTICS OF THE IOWA LYCEUM

The Iowa Lyceum is a five-day, nonresidential summer camp. Each day includes half an hour for breakfast and half an hour for lunch. In addition to the time allotted for meals, there are 20 to 45-minute sessions spread over the week. These sessions have been structured in various formats, but there are five session categories that are standard at each Iowa Lyceum: *Legal, Introducing Philosophizing, Critical Thinking, Student Presentations*, and *Volunteer Sessions*. We discuss each of these in turn.

Legal

The first standard session at the Iowa Lyceum is devoted to safety and legal issues. This is part of University of Iowa policy for programs with minor participants. As a condition of offering the program, the Lyceum founders were required by the university to create a policy manual that includes information on everything from waivers for student drivers to where to flee from a tornado, to make this manual available to students, and to present the most pressing information to participants on the first day.

Introducing Philosophizing

The second standard session is an overview of what philosophizing is. Philosophizing is different from an overview of what *philosophy* is, where the latter would be a description of the areas philosophy comprises, for example, metaphysics, epistemology, existentialism, and so on. The focus of this session is similar to that of a first discussion section in a college introductory philosophy course. The chief aim is to get students talking and thinking philosophically.

To that end, this session is usually led by a copresident who leads an engaging discussion in which a definitional question is raised. Examples include "What is a sandwich?," "What is punch?," "Who is a philosopher?." It turns out that almost everyone in the Iowa Lyceum has a view on these issues. It also turns out that almost everyone in the Iowa Lyceum can produce a counterexample to a proposed answer. This point/counterpoint discussion gets students talking straightaway and through experience introduces them to the common philosophical practice of proposing and evaluating necessary and sufficient conditions of some particular concept: propose necessary and sufficient conditions and give counterexamples to such proposals.

Once students have a grasp of these strategies that philosophers use, like offering necessary and sufficient conditions and giving counterexamples to thought experiments, they are prepared for more substantial philosophical inquiry. Having cut their philosophical teeth on questions like "What is a sandwich?" they then move to weightier questions like "What is political liberty?" Our experience with the Iowa Lyceum has shown that students have no problem moving from playful conceptual questions to serious ones, with just a bit of practice of the common philosophical techniques that are employed to discuss both kinds of questions.

Critical Thinking

The third standard session category comprises three to four distinct individual sessions dedicated to critical thinking. These sessions have taken up myriad topics in logic, for example, the notion of *valid* and *sound* arguments, Frankfurt's notion of *bullshit* and arguing in bad faith, and informal fallacies. We recognize that there are other possibilities for such sessions, however, these sessions have worked for the Iowa Lyceum and the students who attend this Lyceum have enjoyed them.

Student Presentations

Taking place on the fifth day of the camp, the fourth standard session is student-driven. In this session, students work in groups on a topic, philosopher, or text of their choosing. Their choice can be something or someone that/who was discussed during the week or something that requires work outside of what they learned at the Lyceum. Students take two of the back-to-back sessions to put together a presentation of approximately ten minutes each.

Their parents and guardians are invited to join the program for lunch and then see the students give their presentations. Audience members including other students, their parents and guardians, and Lyceum presidents and volunteers are invited to join the camp conversation by asking questions during these presentations or in a question-and-answer period afterward. Organizers usually try to ask questions that let students demonstrate what they learned during the week, and more challenging ones that constructively encourage the presenters to critically evaluate their own work.

Volunteer Sessions

Finally, in addition to the sessions mentioned above, there are ten other daily sessions. These are volunteer sessions, which are led by volunteer teachers, not the camp organizers. Over the years, these sessions have been organized and arranged in different ways. There has been extensive experimentation with the format.

In one iteration, the Iowa Lyceum held two back-to-back sessions focused on discussing either multiple texts or one broad topic. This has been especially effective for comparing texts. One back-to-back session focused first on Plato's *Republic*, then Mill's *On Liberty*. This led to a rich conversation about how different these two thinkers really were.

For example, students were impressed with the similarities between the aristocratic-seeming elevation in Plato's *Republic* of gold-souled philosophers on the one hand and on the other the democratic-seeming elevation in Mill's *Utilitarianism* of the competent judge of pleasures. One student even said aloud during the group discussion of the extent to which Plato's philosopher rulers and Mill's competent judges were similar, "Wow! I never thought of that."

Comparative-style sessions are not the only way to organize back-to-back sessions: volunteers at the Iowa Lyceum have also taught and co-taught debate-style back-to-back sessions. Volunteers often debate constructively, as in an Ethics Bowl, rather than competitively.[2] For example, unlike in a standard debate wherein parties defend opposing positions on a topic, both volunteers presenting back-to-back comparative sessions can defend the same position.

There are many virtues to this format. Students are involved in the discussion while also observing how the professional philosophers leading the session dialogue productively with each other. Of course, volunteers do sometimes disagree, and it can be illuminating for students to observe how considerate, thoughtful interlocutors engage with each other's arguments in a disagreement. The Iowa Lyceum has used the comparative style of session nearly every year because it consistently gets students excited about the topic and encourages careful and precise argumentation. Past sessions in this format have included *The Needs of the Many vs. the Needs of the Few*, *Consequentialism and Special Relationships*, and *Contract Theories of Political Obligations: Hobbes vs. Locke*.

The most common format of a session at the Iowa Lyceum is with one teacher. The formats and content are chosen by the volunteer leading the session. Volunteers all have come to the Iowa Lyceum from the University of

Iowa philosophy department faculty, graduate students, and alumni. The presenter chooses the topic, title, and pedagogical structure of the session. In the past, this autonomy of instructors has resulted in highly positive experiences: instructors have as a rule facilitated wonderful sessions. This overwhelmingly positive experience has supported the strategy of allowing the volunteers at the Iowa Lyceum to keep pedagogical control of their session.

There is one exception to this openness. The Lyceum urges all volunteers to be mindful that the students should do most of the talking. The Iowa Lyceum is a chance for pre-college students to practice philosophizing. The primary goal of the Iowa Lyceum is not to teach a specific content. It has always been to give students practice doing philosophy themselves. Judging from past experience with returning Iowa Lyceum students and their exit surveys, as well as their applications for admission to the Iowa Lyceum, students remember the joy of doing philosophy themselves, not detailed philosophical content particular to some sessions.

The Iowa Lyceum volunteer sessions have typically been organized around a theme, which adds a motif to the conversations for volunteers and for students, helping students connect the ideas they are learning. This has helped boost enrollment in the Iowa Lyceum, as the different themes give returning students a fresh collection of philosophical topics, authors, and texts. Themes are also useful in advertising the Iowa Lyceum to parents, as a list of ten session titles is hardly digestible, and an overly broad scope leaves too much to the imagination. Past themes include *Science and Technology, History of Philosophy, Philosophy and Society,* and *Philosophy and Politics.*

Importantly, the themes have always been merely a guide and organizational tool. The Iowa Lyceum has never rejected a topic that a volunteer has wanted to teach simply because it did not fit that year's theme. The Iowa Lyceum is always grateful for the time volunteers give. It has generally not insisted upon a specific topic, author, or text. And usually, the themes chosen are very broad. This allows almost any topic to fit under it.

DEPENDABLE FINANCIAL AND COMMUNITY SUPPORT

The expenses for the Iowa Lyceum come to approximately $2,000. The largest expense is food: the program provides a light breakfast and hearty lunch for students, volunteers, and organizers. The Iowa Lyceum's practice includes providing shirts for students, organizers, and volunteers. Additionally, the Iowa Lyceum has also been able to provide philosophy books for students, which serves two purposes. First, students can take the books home and continue reading philosophy; second, the books can be used for group discussion during the Iowa Lyceum week.

Even with these expenses, $2,000 is a low financial cost for providing access to so much philosophy. There is one chief reason that the Iowa Lyceum can provide so much philosophy within such a small budget: neither the organizers nor the volunteers are paid nor have they ever asked for payment. Although we make a formal staff distinction between organizers and volunteers, everyone who participates as a staff member in the Iowa Lyceum volunteers their time. They all share a commitment to the importance of promoting precollege philosophy and of the intrinsic value of the Iowa Lyceum.

Yet even with these minimal expenses and even with our staff volunteering their time, external funding is still so crucial. The Iowa Lyceum offers the camp entirely free to students. In 2019, we had twenty-four students. Dividing the cost evenly among them in the form of a registration fee would have resulted in billing them about $85 each. In years with fewer students, the figure could be double that, or $170 each. This cost would be a significant barrier for many families. In a country in which precollege philosophy is difficult to access, we wanted to eliminate as many barriers as possible.

The Iowa Lyceum has had enthusiastic financial support from a variety of offices of the University of Iowa since the Lyceum's first year. These offices have included the College of Liberal Arts and Sciences, the Division of Continuing Education, the Office of the Provost, and the Department of Philosophy. University administration has been excited about a non-STEM camp for young people since the Lyceum's founders first pitched the idea in 2012.

The program's expenses have been covered by various units of the University of Iowa. In 2018, the Iowa Lyceum also received external grant support from both the Philosophy Learning and Teaching Organization (PLATO) and the American Philosophical Association (APA). These internal and external funding agencies are listed here in the hope that it will inspire the reader to investigate funding opportunities for a new or continuing precollege philosophy program elsewhere.

The best friends of the Iowa Lyceum are local teachers and parents. Teachers especially have been helpful in spreading the word about the program to students they expect will be interested. The Iowa Lyceum usually e-mails area teachers at junior high and high schools several months before the application deadline for participants. The Lyceum also sends e-mails to past participants, who have helped in advertising the program to their younger peers.

This person-to-person advertising approach has ensured that the Iowa Lyceum has grown each year, as by far the most effective marketing of the program to new students is word-of-mouth. This community support, combined with a regularly updated website, has nearly eliminated the need for the typical advertising costs for summer programs. The program is grateful to students, parents, and teachers for their enthusiastic and vital promotion of the Iowa Lyceum.

PEDAGOGY OF THE IOWA LYCEUM

The pedagogical focus of the Iowa Lyceum is on the student-led learning and practice of philosophy. That approach is manifested in the heavy use of discussion, debate, guided critical reading and textual analysis, games, and student presentations at the end of the camp period. Some amount of lecture is often needed to lay groundwork for understanding a particular issue, but the Lyceum instructors minimize this use of lecture as much as possible and work to put student discussion at the center of their own learning.

In order to maintain the high standard of teaching the program organizers desire for Lyceum, the organizers have typically restricted the invitations to teach a Lyceum session to only those volunteers who have demonstrated undergraduate teaching experience. Organizers almost always discuss a newer instructor's lesson plan before the session. Using these guidelines helps maintain an intellectually stimulating environment for Lyceum participants. In the case of the Iowa Lyceum the teaching standard is easy to maintain, since the volunteers come from the University of Iowa's Department of Philosophy. Almost everyone in the department teaches every semester, making it easy to find volunteers with significant teaching experience.

The Iowa Lyceum's practice has been to ask faculty members to volunteer before asking graduate students to do so, as they are typically the most experienced teachers. Graduate students who are asked to teach have often led discussion sections for two years, and sometimes have been the instructor of record for one year. Often these instructors, besides doing annual departmental teaching orientations, have also done teaching practicums and certificate programs with the Center for Teaching at the University of Iowa.

Instructors with at least this much teaching experience at the college level generally find the transition to teaching a self-selected group of engaged pre-college students easy and fulfilling: discussions are very easy to get going with such a group, and they readily engage each other's points in group discussion, partly because they are thrilled to be discussing philosophy with like-minded peers. Instructors have had next to no difficulties teaching precollege students as compared with college students: students do get bored if the presenter talks for an extended period without inviting discussion. If anything, the impact of teaching at the Iowa Lyceum has made instructors reflect on how to facilitate more discussion in their college-level courses.

STUDENT ENROLLMENT AND DEMOGRAPHICS OF THE IOWA LYCEUM

Enrollment

The Iowa Lyceum determines its enrollment through an electronic application that students complete and submit via e-mail by approximately one month before the summer program begins. The application is hosted on the program's website, to which the various advertising messages about the Lyceum direct interested students. The application asks for basic personal information and how the applicant heard of the Lyceum.

The applicants are also asked to write a detailed paragraph describing why the student wants to participate in the program. The founders expected that by asking students to submit a thoughtful reflective piece about the program, even if it is short, only interested students would apply. Perhaps as a result, the program has historically accepted everyone who has submitted a complete application, and all but a few accepted students have participated in the program.

Demographics

The demographic information for the Iowa Lyceum's students is all self-reported. Except for enrollment information, most of the demographic data comes from our 2018 program, which was the first year in which we began collecting such information.

Age: The age of the participants was between fourteen and seventeen years.

Geography: Of these twenty-four students, one was from Minnesota. A student in California also applied, but was unable to attend due to an inability to secure housing. The students from Iowa come from six different schools in the Johnson County area.

Ethnicity: Of the twenty-four students, one self-reported as Hispanic/Latino. Nine self-reported as Not-Hispanic/Latino. The remainder did not self-report.

Race: Of the twenty-four students, one self-reported as Asian. One self-reported as black or African American. Eleven self-reported as White. The remainder did not self-report. Three categories had no self-reports: American Indian or Alaska Native, Native Hawaiian or Other Pacific Islander, and Other.

Gender: Of the twenty-four students, two self-reported as Female. Twelve self-reported as Male. The remainder did not self-report. Three categories had no self-reports: Nonbinary, Non-identifying, and Other.

Enrollment: 2013: eight students, 2014: nine students, 2015: fifteen students, 2016: eighteen students, 2017: eleven students, 2018: twenty-five students. Several students enroll in the Lyceum more than once. The 2018 Iowa Lyceum had five returning students from the 2017 program, one of whom had also attended the 2016 program. The 2016 program had seven returning students from the 2015 program, two of whom had been in the 2014 program. This large number of repeat students, ranging from 20 percent to 33 percent, and four consecutive years of double-digit enrollment are highly encouraging signs that the Iowa Lyceum is here to stay.

Organizers: All organizers of the Iowa Lyceum have been graduate students. Having two to three people has been sufficient to organize the program. Past presidents who are no longer graduate students have also generously donated their time to the Iowa Lyceum by teaching sessions, taking pictures, and offering logistical advice and suggestions. The organizers of the Iowa

Lyceum have to date all been white, excepting one student organizer in 2017. The two founders were both male, and the subsequent three organizers were also male. The current president is female, as are the copresidents for the 2019 program.

WHY DO THE IOWA LYCEUM?

This chapter is written with the hope that others will start Lyceum programs. The chapter includes information that the authors think will help with organizing and operating a program. The above information describes the nuts and bolts of how we "do" the Iowa Lyceum. It does not explain why one should start a Lyceum program. So why should one start a Lyceum?

First, organizing a Lyceum is easy. As a nonresidential camp, it does not take much time. It does not take much money, even when it is free to students. It can run on just $2,000. Many institutions of higher education are willing to support such an outreach effort on that budget. Many professional organizations that promote philosophy are willing to fund a Lyceum, too.

Second, organizing a Lyceum advertises philosophy widely. The Iowa Lyceum has gotten press from "Daily Nous," "Iowa Now," and *The Daily Iowan*. PLATO and the APA have funded the Iowa Lyceum and advertised this funding on their respective websites. Word has gotten out nationally about the program, in large part thanks to these funding agencies and to the energy of its founders and presidents communicating with the outlets mentioned previously.

These forms of communication include recording videos promoting the program, conducting interviews about their precollege philosophy endeavors, sharing information about the program through various social media outlets, and even writing a book chapter about the Iowa Lyceum. The results have been felt locally. Alumni of the Iowa Lyceum have enrolled in introductory philosophy courses at the University of Iowa before graduating high school.

Third, the program is exciting and meaningful for students. Below are some excerpts from students' anonymous exit surveys after the 2018 Iowa Lyceum. The prompting question was, "Would you recommend the Lyceum to others or not? Why or why not?" Here is a sampling of what the students said:

"Yes! It was educational, engaging, and sparked my curiosity in the subject. Now I have more ideas on what to read this summer."

"Yes I would because I think there was a very good, intelligent crowd that came that contributed and seemed to come here for the learning. There were also a lot of interesting things I learned."

"Yes, because it's fun, there's food, and it changed the way I think."

"Yes, because it really expands the mind and challenges it to face different perspectives, it's a good experience."

"Yes, it's very interesting and it's amazing to hear what people have to say."

Notice the recurring theme—that students really appreciated the discussion. They enjoyed engaging philosophically with their peers and appreciated how the Iowa Lyceum changed how they see things.

This kind of engagement in an atmosphere created specifically for this kind of engagement is rare for precollege students in the United States, as precollege philosophy courses and programs are scarce in American public schools. The Iowa Lyceum students often report in their exit surveys that their experience in the Iowa Lyceum is their first time doing philosophy. That is no doubt part of the reason why students treasure it: they can see the impact these discussions have on them individually, so participants often reenroll in subsequent years, participating in the Iowa Lyceum two and sometimes three times.

The value to students is truly the main reason to organize an Iowa Lyceum. Aristotle rightly said that when one teaches successfully, the change occurs in the learner: "To teach will be the same as to learn. . . . Teaching is the activity of a person who can teach, yet the operation is performed in something . . ." (*Physics* 202b). This is especially true when one teaches philosophy. Over 2,000 years later, Bertrand Russell made a related point. He noted that science is useful instrumentally even to those that do not study it. Philosophy, in contrast, does not have this utility. Its utility is "through its effects on the lives of those who study it" (*Problems* 288).

Philosophers often give instrumental justifications for why studying philosophy is good. The profession advertises enhanced critical thinking ability, improved civil discourse, increased empathy from considering the merits of other's views, higher scores on standardized tests like the LSAT and GMAT, and so on.

This kind of instrumental justification for philosophy outreach relies on further claims that themselves depend upon empirical justification—for example, statistical evidence that the study of philosophy really does improve LSAT scores and the further claim that the students in question presently and in the future want to be lawyers—and it would be a mistake to hold the value of philosophy wholly hostage to everchanging practical demands and to individual choices applicable to only some students.

A stronger rationale for philosophy outreach is that professional philosophers are capable of engaging in this kind of outreach, particularly in the summer months when schedules are freer, and that the study of philosophy is intrinsically good: it is personally and intellectually enriching for the student. As Bertrand Russell suggests, studying philosophy encourages a healthy skepticism of one's beliefs and appreciation for the subtlety of the philosophical questions that philosophy invites us to pursue:

> The value of philosophy is, in fact, to be sought largely in its very uncertainty. The man who has no tincture of philosophy goes through life imprisoned in the prejudices derived from common sense, from the habitual beliefs of his age or his nation, and from convictions which have grown up in his mind without the co-operation or consent of his deliberate reason. To such a man the world tends to become definite, finite, obvious; common objects rouse no questions, and unfamiliar possibilities are contemptuously rejected. As soon as we begin to philosophize, on the contrary, we find . . . that even the most everyday things lead to problems to which only very incomplete answers can be given. Philosophy, though unable to tell us with certainty what is the true answer to the doubts which it raises, is able to suggest many possibilities which enlarge our thoughts and free them from the tyranny of custom. Thus, while diminishing our feeling of certainty as to what things are, it greatly increases our knowledge as to what they may be; it removes the somewhat arrogant dogmatism of those who have never travelled into the region of liberating doubt, and it keeps alive our sense of wonder by showing familiar things in an unfamiliar aspect. (*The Problems of Philosophy* [1912]: 242–244)

Like Russell, we think philosophy should be studied for the betterment of its students:

> Philosophy is to be studied, not for the sake of any definite answers to its questions since no definite answers can, as a rule, be known to be true, but rather for the sake of the questions themselves; because these questions enlarge our conception of what is possible, enrich our intellectual imagination and diminish

the dogmatic assurance which closes the mind against speculation; but above all because, through the greatness of the universe which philosophy contemplates, the mind also is rendered great, and becomes capable of that union with the universe which constitutes its highest good. (*Problems* 249–250)[3]

This is the real reason to do a Lyceum program, and the ultimate reason why we have done so. These reasons are particularly compelling for a precollege philosophy camp in the United States, where it is rare to philosophize with peers and instructors who love wisdom, too. The Iowa Lyceum is a manifestation of the University of Iowa philosophy department's conscious choice to offer the benefits of philosophy to younger neighbors and future peers and voters that would otherwise be deprived of philosophy's intellectual riches and moral betterment.

NOTES

1. Kris Phillips now directs the Utah Lyceum. See his chapter in *Growing Up with Philosophy Camp: How Learning to Think Develops Friendship, Community, and a Sense of Self*, edited by Claire Elise Katz, 111–120 (Rowman and Littlefield, 2020).

2. "Ethics Bowl" refers to national debate competitions in the style favored by the Intercollegiate Ethics Bowl and the National High School Ethics Bowl. In these Ethics Bowl competitions, student debate teams review cases and prepare arguments in favor of the position(s) the team endorses. Competing teams can both argue for the same proposition, and it is in this sense that Ethics Bowl debates are cooperative rather than competitive, even though there are winners and losers. The National High School Ethics Bowl maintains a webpage at http://www.nhseb.unc.edu and the Intercollegiate Ethics Bowl page is at http://www.appe-ethics.org/ethics-bowl.

3. See Bertrand Russell, *The Problems of Philosophy*, 1912 edition, Archive.org. The edition we used is available here: https://archive.org/details/problemsofphilo00russuoft/page/242.

Chapter 4

The Philosophy and Critical Thinking (PACT) Summer Camp at Ohio State

James Fritz, Lavender McKittrick-Sweitzer, Justin D'Arms, and Julia Jorati

The Department of Philosophy at the Ohio State University launched the Philosophy and Critical Thinking (PACT) summer day camp for high school students in 2017. Several motivations contributed to this idea. First, few high schools offer philosophy classes, yet this age group is well-suited to enjoy and benefit from exposure to philosophical thinking and discussion.

Second, the organizers hoped that exposing diverse groups of high school students to philosophy might help diversify the undergraduate philosophy programs at Ohio State and other universities. At least anecdotally, this has worked quite well so far.

A third reason was to provide summer funding and a different type of teaching experience for philosophy graduate students at Ohio State. Aside from these pragmatic benefits, instructors find this work incredibly rewarding as they see the hopes the next generation has to make the world a better place, and are reminded of the bright-eyed curiosity they experienced when they first discovered philosophy themselves.

Student reviews were extremely favorable from the start, and it became clear that there is a large appetite for this sort of intellectual experience on a college campus in the central Ohio community. Since then, the camp has grown by about half each year: there were twenty-three participants in 2017, thirty-nine in 2018, and sixty-one in 2019. Its future seems bright.

PACT is run primarily by philosophy graduate and advanced undergraduate students with a faculty leader. Campers work with instructors on small-group activities, projects and discussions, and convene for larger sessions with visiting faculty from time to time. In what follows, PACT's programs are explained in detail, and some information is provided about logistics that may be helpful to other camps at early developmental stages.

THE ELEMENTS OF A WEEK AT CAMP

Ohio State's PACT summer camp offers a variety of experiences designed to be engaging, memorable, and philosophically rigorous. This section describes some of those experiences and explains how they complement and reinforce one another.

Yearly Theme

Each summer, the PACT summer camp is designed to focus on a specific philosophical topic. In 2017, the camp's theme was "Rights and Liberty"; in 2018, the theme was "Justice"; and in 2019, the theme was "Identity." These topics are chosen with an eye to several criteria. First, is the topic likely to be immediately interesting to a wide range of high schoolers, even those with no background in philosophy? Second, does the topic lend itself to a wide variety of activities, puzzles, and applications? Third, will this topic provide a useful introduction to the methods, goals, and ideas typical of philosophy as a discipline?

Foundational or central philosophical ideas that concern the theme at hand are introduced early in the week, so that later activities can build on those foundational ideas. For instance, when the camp's theme was "Rights and Liberty," the first day of camp featured an introduction to the distinction between *negative* rights (e.g., the right not to be attacked) and *positive* rights (e.g., the right to health care).

Nearly all of the camp's sessions are devoted to activities that concern the yearly theme. Those activities, generally, fall into five categories: *debates*, *student-led research*, *lessons*, *guest presentations*, and *enrichment activities*. The remainder of this section describes how PACT summer camp instructors have used each of these activities to introduce campers to philosophy.

Debates

A week at PACT summer camp features two units devoted to formal debates, whose purpose it is for students to practice argumentation and to delve more deeply into a philosophical question. The first of the two debates is held on Wednesday and helps students to become comfortable with debate in a comparatively low-stakes context; it also gives students a chance to learn from feedback on their performance. The second debate, which is held during the showcase on Fridays, serves as a powerful capstone experience for camp: working together in teams, students draw on everything they have learned over the course of the week to offer and critique philosophical arguments.

Debates are kicked off through a lesson that provides shared context for the discussion to follow. For instance, in 2018, students prepared for a debate on affirmative action by watching and discussing two videos: one documenting persistent wealth inequality between racial groups in America and one describing a recent Supreme Court case challenging Ivy League admission practices.

Establishing this shared context, students are then randomly assigned to debate teams. In their teams, they get two additional hours to prepare for the debate, coached by camp instructors. Each team uses print anthologies or online resources to locate and evaluate existing arguments. They share their findings with each other and use them to prepare for their distinct roles in debate.

Each student on a debate team plays at least one of three roles: providing an opening statement, rebutting the opposing team's opening statement, or responding to the opposing team's rebuttal. Each of these roles corresponds to a single "round" of debate in which representatives of both teams speak. Between rounds of debate, teams regroup and prepare for the next round together. After the three rounds of debate, students debrief, discussing their performances in a positive, constructive way. No victor is declared; rather, students are encouraged to reflect on what they learned, what each team did well, and what each team should change for future debates. This exercise has provided our students with an exciting and intellectually rigorous opportunity to engage in depth with specific philosophical discussions.

STUDENT-LED RESEARCH

Early in the week—soon after students have become familiar with the overarching theme for the week—students consider a list of topics that raise interesting philosophical questions related to the week's theme. For instance, in 2018, the camp's theme was Justice, and students were offered the following list:

- Charity
- Drug legalization
- Environmental justice
- Genetic enhancement
- Gun law
- Health care
- Immigration
- Inheritance tax
- Judicial activism
- Justice as a personality trait
- Mandatory minimum sentences
- Mass incarceration
- Moral luck (Can whether you are a morally good person depend on luck?)
- Polygamy
- Public school funding
- Punishment
- Justifications for punishment
- Free will and punishment
- Reparations for slavery
- Universal basic income
- Voter ID laws
- War
- Or, pick your own topic

Students express preferences as to which of these topics to research. On the basis of these preferences, they form small groups (typically between two and four students); over the course of the week, these groups look into the existing philosophical literature about a shared topic. This exercise gives students control over an important aspect of their learning at camp, and it has frequently been one of the camp experiences about which students feel most passionate.

Student-led research occurs in three stages. First, students (with significant help from camp instructors) look into existing philosophical arguments on the topic that they have chosen. They share arguments with group members, evaluate those arguments together, and sometimes, aim to create arguments of their own.

Second, students choose just one argument about their shared topic, and they analyze that argument's virtues and vices in depth. This may be an argument that they have found in the existing literature or it may be an original argument they have created together. Third, they create a presentation that shares their in-depth analysis of their chosen argument. The presentation must clearly formulate the argument, explain why the argument might be appealing, consider objections to the argument, and consider at least one response to an objection.

PACT campers have let their creativity shine in sharing presentations about their small-group research. Some students have created technically impressive (and often very funny) videos; others have designed attractive, engaging posters. Whatever their form, these presentations play a starring role in the final camp experience: a showcase to which campers' parents and guardians as well as guest speakers are invited. In 2018 and 2019, the creators of the best video presentations—chosen by campers and parents or guardians—received prizes at the showcase.

LESSONS

When an idea or a skill is absolutely vital for mature philosophical engagement with the year's theme, instructors design lessons that help campers to master that idea or skill. For instance, since much of a week at camp is spent considering and analyzing arguments, one early lesson is always devoted to the basics of logic and argumentation. Through lively, interesting examples and small-group practice, instructors introduce students to the notions of premise and conclusion, validity and soundness, objection and response.

Few lessons involve any sustained lecture component, and many of them prominently feature creative, engaging activities. For instance, in 2018's justice-themed camp, one-hour-long lesson was devoted to clarifying and discussing the notion of epistemic injustice. (This is the notion that someone can be wronged in their capacity as a knower; for example, it is unjust to take someone's ideas or claims less seriously because of their gender or race.) This session was primarily devoted to the performance and discussion of pre-written skits that illustrated the phenomenon of epistemic injustice.

To take another example: one session considered issues of justice associated with racial profiling; it was structured like a courtroom drama, with some students playing the part of lawyers and other students playing the role of jurors.[1] In both of these cases, playacting helped students to become comfortable with one another and provided a springboard into sustained, often passionate philosophical discussion. In anonymous surveys, several students cited these lessons as their favorite camp experiences.

When the camp became larger, most lessons took place in smaller groups or "pods," allowing students to receive more individualized attention from instructors and to have more productive discussions. Ensuring that students are engaging in productive discussions throughout the camp is of the utmost importance, given the dialogical nature of philosophy. PACT discussions are often based on some kind of prompt, such as a thought experiment, a real-life case, a fictional dialogue, a game, or a clip from a TV show. Instructors facilitate discussions during each activity by posing open-ended questions about the philosophical issue at hand, and students provide responses, based on personal experiences, intuitions, or prior knowledge.

Mixing lessons on theoretical issues with lessons on applied questions allows students to apply the philosophical theories they have already learned to concrete cases and reflect on their plausibility. Since students come from diverse backgrounds, discussions typically include multiple perspectives on a given issue, with the instructors facilitating constructive and respectful dialogue between those with disagreements. By participating in discussions of this sort, students are able to appreciate that resolving a philosophical issue comes with addressing numerous considerations, as well as realize that they share more common ground with those they disagree with than they may have initially thought.

GUEST PRESENTATIONS

One of PACT's greatest resources is the talented group of faculty and graduate students associated with Ohio State. Many have kindly volunteered to offer guest presentations that help students to think in depth about a philosophical topic that relates closely to the week's theme. For instance, in 2017's Rights-and-Liberty themed camp, faculty members visited camp to lead learning experiences concerning immigration and sanctuary cities, the paradox of deontology, John Stuart Mill's "harm principle," and animal rights.

It is worth flagging that "presentation" may be a misnomer; many guest-led experiences are highly interactive. For instance, in 2017, Amy Shuster led students on a mini field trip to an art exhibit on global human migration in order to prepare students to think about the ethics of legal restrictions on migration. And in 2018, Tristram McPherson illustrated the prisoner's dilemma by having students play against one another for cookies. In short, guest instructors have done a fabulous job sculpting experiences that are both philosophically rigorous and highly engaging for campers.

Enrichment Activities

Some camp experiences take students outside the classroom and into a new mode of learning about philosophy. For instance, in 2018, all PACT campers were given the option to participate in a virtual-reality simulation of Judith Jarvis Thomson's "bystander-at-the-switch" thought experiment. In this simulation, each student was put in the position of choosing whether to flip a switch so that an out-of-control trolley veered onto a sidetrack, killing one, or to leave the switch alone, effectively leaving five (virtual!) people in the path of the trolley to die. Students loved this experience, and the ensuing discussion of the ethics of killing and letting die was both animated and highly reflective.

To take another example: each year, PACT summer camp sets aside some time to watch a movie or TV show episodes that raise interesting philosophical questions related to that year's theme. In 2017, for instance, campers watched *The Truman Show*. They then proceeded to discuss questions that the movie raises about rights (Could a benefit to Truman's well-being justify the infringement on his right to privacy?) and liberty (Are there any genuine restrictions on Truman's liberty that aren't also present in your life?).

In 2018, they watched the first three episodes of the TV show *The Good Place* and discussed the justice or injustice of the system for punishment and reward that the TV show depicts. In 2019, they watched the first episode and some other clips from the TV show *Switched at Birth* and discussed issues such as disability identity, ethnic identity, and genetic identity.

A WEEK AT CAMP

Every day, students arrive on campus by 9:00 a.m. and depart at 4:00 p.m. For lunch, campers go to dining halls on campus or to nearby restaurants in small groups with instructors. They receive temporary ID cards from Ohio State with which they can pay for their meals. On the last day, lunch takes the form of a catered picnic on the main quad with lawn games. There is no homework; campers are sometimes asked to read short texts, but that happens during the camp.

The schedule below shows how the diverse array of camp activities come together into a cohesive whole. Monday's activities primarily serve to orient students to camp, to philosophy, and to the week's theme. Tuesday allows students to prepare for the first debate and to deepen their understanding of the week's theme. The first debate is scheduled for Wednesday; a significant portion of that day is also devoted to student-led research. Thursday allows students to move toward the final stages of their research projects. On Friday, students prepare for the final debate and finalize their research; both are shared with parents and guardians at a final showcase event.

Within this overall structure, PACT summer camp instructors facilitate fun and interesting experiences of all sorts—including engaging lessons, virtual-reality experiences, movie viewing, and even a picnic on Friday. In short, there is never a dull moment at PACT summer camp; the camp both entertains and engages students while supporting them in multiple sustained academic endeavors.

EXAMPLE DAILY SCHEDULE

Monday
9:00–9:35 a.m.	An introduction to camp
9:40–10:15 a.m.	Lesson: disagreement and the truth
10:20–10:55 a.m.	Game: different kinds of justice
11:00–11:55 a.m.	Lesson: logic and arguments
12:00–1:15 p.m.	Lunch
1:15–1:55 p.m.	Introduction to weeklong video project
2:00–2:55 p.m.	Guest instructor: Eric MacGilvray on luck egalitarianism
3:00–4:00 p.m.	Scavenger hunt!

Tuesday
9:00–9:55 a.m.	Introduction to debate 1: affirmative action
10:00–10:55 a.m.	Research for debate 1
11:00–11:55 a.m.	Video project work time
12:00–1:15 p.m.	Lunch
1:15–2:55 p.m.	Metro Library trip (combined with research for debate 1)
3:00–4:00 p.m.	Guest instructor: Tristram McPherson on complicity in large collective injustices

Wednesday
9:00–9:55 a.m.	Debate 1: affirmative action
10:00–10:55 a.m.	Lesson: epistemic injustice
11:00 AM–12:00 p.m.	Guest instructor: Amy Shuster on restorative justice
12:00–1:00 p.m.	Lunch
1:00–3:00 p.m.	Virtual-reality thought experiment (alternating with video project work time)
3:00–4:00 p.m.	Discussion of virtual-reality thought experiment

Thursday
9:00–10:00 a.m.	Final preparations for video recording time
10:00–11:55 a.m.	Video recording (and editing) time
12:00–1:30 p.m.	Lunch and movie
1:30–2:00 p.m.	Movie discussion
2:00–3:00 p.m.	Guest instructor: Don Hubin on justice and future generations
3:00–4:00 p.m.	Activity: justice and different kinds of evidence

Friday
9:00–10:00 a.m.	Introduction to debate 2: animal personhood
10:00–11:00 a.m.	Preparation for debate 2
11:00–11:55 a.m.	Lesson: global justice
12:00–1:15 p.m.	Lunch and picnic
1:15–2:15 p.m.	Final preparations for debate 2
2:15–2:45 p.m.	Final discussion, exit survey
2:45–3:30 p.m.	Debate 2
3:30–4:00 p.m.	Showcase: Student video presentations! Parents welcome.

Demographics and Admissions

The camp has grown every year since it started in 2017. In the first year, there were thirty-four applicants, of which twenty-three attended camp. In 2018, fifty-eight students applied and thirty-nine attended. In 2019, seventy-four applied and sixty-one attended. The discrepancy between applications and participants is not due to a competitive admissions process but rather due to the fact that some students applied but then decided not to attend. PACT has so far admitted every applicant who met the basic requirements, that is, every applicant who is of the right age and has a positive academic recommendation letter.

So far, the applicant pools and the camp participants have been quite diverse in multiple dimensions—much more diverse than the profession of philosophy and also much more diverse than the average philosophy class at Ohio State. Below are some basic demographic data about the participants in the first three years. The data were gathered at the time these participants applied for the camp (figures 4.1–4.5).

	2017	2018	2019
African American/Black	20.83%	10.26%	18.03%
Asian/Asian American	4.17%	7.69%	21.31%
Caucasian/White	41.67%	53.85%	27.87%
Hispanic/Latinx	0.00%	5.13%	1.64%
Indian	8.33%	0.00%	0.00%
Middle Eastern	0.00%	0.00%	1.64%
Native American	0.00%	2.56%	0.00%
Biracial/Mixed	12.50%	7.69%	1.64%
Unreported	12.50%	12.82%	27.87%

FINANCING PACT

As the demographic information above indicates, PACT has been growing quickly. There seems to be considerable interest in the community. Much of the increase is due to a growing reputation with school counselors and camp alumni. The high quality of instruction has probably been an important factor in accounting for the positive experiences that campers report.

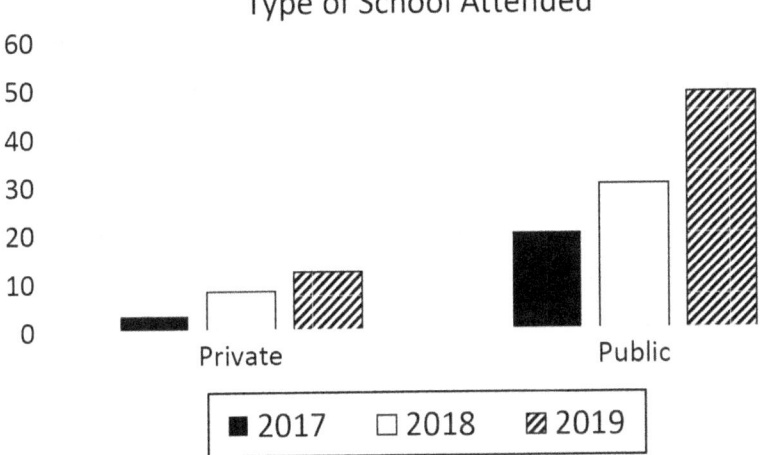

Figure 4.1   Participant's Type of School.

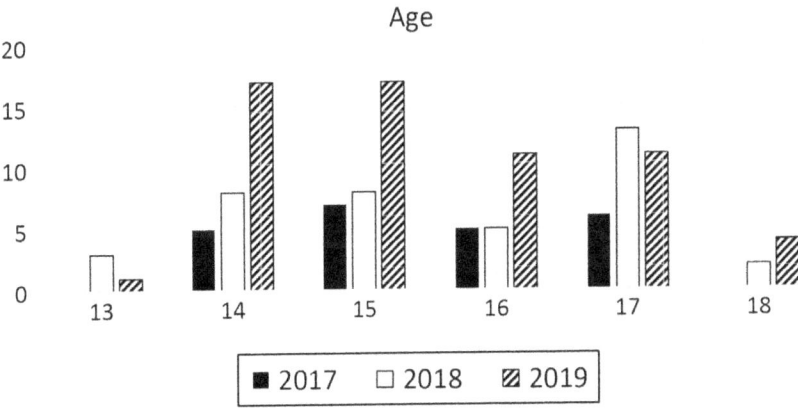

Figure 4.2   Participant's Age.

From the start, the organizers have tried to keep the ratio of students to instructors low, both for pedagogical reasons and because one explicit goal of the camp for the philosophy department has been to provide summer funding for more philosophy graduate students. Accordingly, about 75 percent of the costs associated with PACT come from instructor salaries. Other costs include recruitment, food, teaching materials, T-shirts, and other freebies for campers, as well as legally required background checks on everyone working directly with minors.

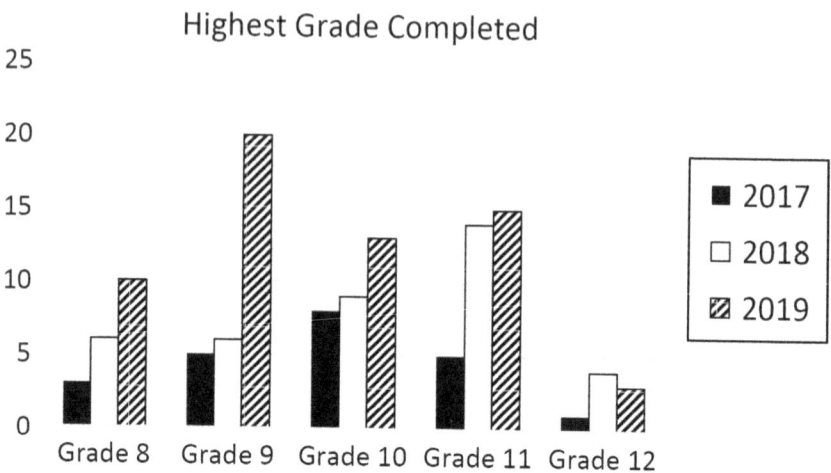

Figure 4.3 Participant's Most Recently Completed Grade.

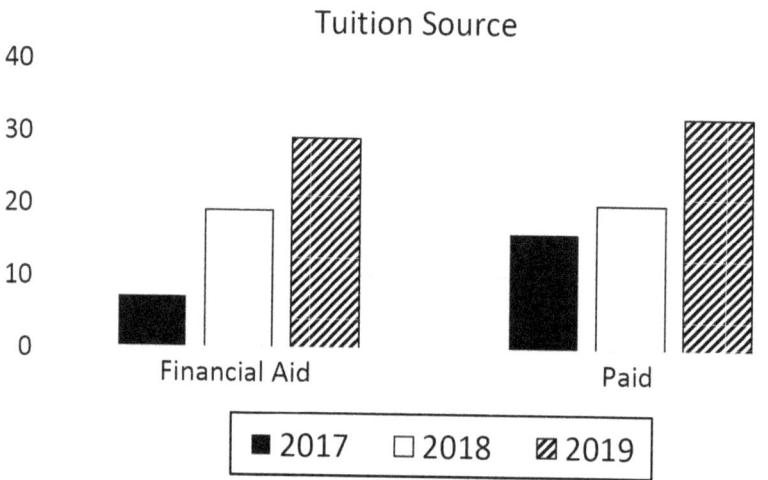

Figure 4.4 Student's Tuition Source.

PACT is funded by tuition, supplemented by modest support from the Ohio State University Philosophy department and, recently, by a grant from the Ohio State University Office of Engagement. Tuition has been $350 since the beginning of the camp. In the first year, almost all the campers paid tuition. In order to increase the diversity of the camp, and create opportunities for students who could not afford it, PACT leadership looked for grant support from various sources, including local foundations, the American Philosophical Association (APA), and the university.

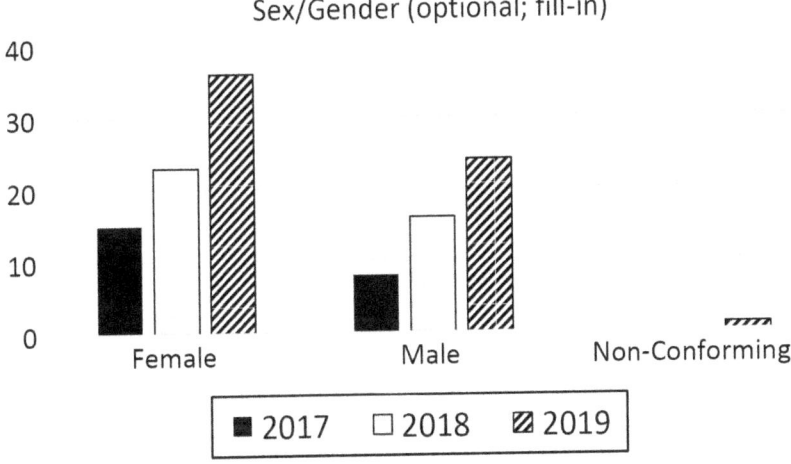

Figure 4.5 Student's Sex/Gender (Optional).

In the second year of camp, many more students applied, and active efforts were undertaken to recruit students who would need scholarships to attend. A grant of $16,000 from OSU for two years made it possible to admit roughly equal numbers of paying and scholarship students in 2018 and 2019. The university also provided free space and some staff support to receive and process payments.

Although PACT was fortunate enough to receive grant support, one challenge to doing so may apply as well to other camps: the motivations for supporting a program of this kind are diverse. They include expanding the reach of philosophy, improving critical thinking in high school students, providing scholarships to increase the economic, racial, and ethnic diversity of the campers, and (for the organizers, at least) supporting philosophy graduate students. No one funder was interested in all of these goals. The APA was the only organization with an obvious stake in the first goal, and funders whose main interest is in providing opportunities for socioeconomically disadvantaged groups did not tend to see our program as the best outlet for their interests.

Finally, education-focused funders with some potential interest in supporting improvements to critical thinking among high school students wanted clearer evidence of the lasting impact of this sort of program than was available as these applications were being written. Grant-writers seeking support for this sort of work will have to think carefully about how to thread this needle.

SERVICE-LEARNING COURSE

The Ohio State Philosophy Department also offers a service-learning course called "Teaching Philosophy" that has benefits for the summer camp; in 2018 and 2019, it was taught by PACT's faculty adviser Julia Jorati. The course is open to advanced undergraduates as well as graduate students and is typically offered in the spring semester.

Students in the course learn about pedagogy and teaching techniques, reflect on how to introduce secondary school students to philosophy, and design engaging philosophy lessons for high school students. They also teach a few of their lessons at a local public high school. The learning goals of this course include acquiring basic teaching skills and gaining a new perspective on the discipline of philosophy. This course benefits PACT in several ways.

First, the course provides training for potential PACT instructors. After all, students who have completed this course will know, better than most others, how to design and teach effective philosophy lessons aimed at high school students. When hiring staff for the camp, the faculty organizers view completion of the service-learning course favorably, even though it is not a requirement. Most of the graduate student PACT instructors have completed the service-learning course. Moreover, a few undergraduates from the service-learning course have helped with the camp in 2018 and 2019, either as volunteers or as paid instructors.

A second way in which the service-learning course benefits PACT is by providing lesson plan ideas. At least one week of the course is devoted explicitly to gathering ideas for the summer camp. Students read philosophical literature about the year's theme and jointly develop a few activities and lessons based on this literature.

For instance, for the theme "Identity," the students read W. E. B. Du Bois's "Of Our Spiritual Strivings" and then worked in groups to come up with lessons on the concept of double consciousness. They also watched the first episode of the TV show *Switched at Birth* and came up with ways to discuss themes from this show, such as disability pride, genetic identity, and ethnic identity. Moreover, one of the written assignments for the course is a full lesson plan for the summer camp, on that year's theme. Some of these plans are then used for the summer camp.

Finally, the service-learning course has also benefited PACT through a research project conducted by Corey Keyser, one of the undergraduate students in the course, during the 2018 summer camp. His study aimed to investigate whether the camp improves the participants' critical thinking, argumentation, and public speaking skills. Keyser used pre- and post-surveys to assess critical thinking skills; he also analyzed the students' performance in the two debates in order to assess argumentation and public speaking skills. The study found that there were statistically significant improvements in all three categories.

CONCLUSION

In short, PACT has been a great success. OSU has made strides toward achieving each of the four goals that served as motivating reasons for establishing the camp: exposing high school students to philosophy in an effort to improve their critical thinking skills, diversifying and bolstering the discipline at the undergraduate level, improving the funding situation for graduate students, and expanding the pedagogical opportunities of graduate (and advanced undergraduate) students. As PACT's reach continues to grow throughout mid-Ohio, there are reasons to be optimistic that the program is creating a lasting positive effect upon participants, instructors, and the discipline more widely.

NOTE

1. The full text of this courtroom activity can be found in chapter 8 of the book.

Chapter 5

Philosophy Summer Camp
A Philosophical World of Tangible Conversations

Kimberly Arriaga-Gonzalez,
Cristina Cammarano, and Jackson Malkus

The Philosophy Summer Camp at Salisbury University (SU)[1] is a weeklong day camp for high school students from local public schools. It was first offered in June 2018 with support from the Fulton School of Liberal Arts and generous funding provided by the Whiting Foundation. The camp is now a regular offering included in the department's yearly activities with support from the dean's office.

   The intent animating the camp springs from the belief that academic philosophy benefits from serious and non-patronizing collaboration with the local community, and the local community as well benefits from regular exchanges with philosophy students and faculty. From what we observed in our experience with the camp, the high school students attending the camp (from now on, campers) and the college students facilitating the activities (from now on, teaching fellows) found an invaluable source of joy and motivation in the shared experience of philosophical community formed through the camp experience.

PARTICIPANTS

The campers were selected through a process that asked teachers to nominate students who showed potential and could thrive in a camp like ours.

These students then completed an application in which they were asked to write responses to short essay questions about their interest in and motivation toward philosophy. Because of funding, we could accommodate twenty campers, of which sixteen were rising seniors, three were rising juniors, and one was a rising eighth grader.

With the exception of two campers, all others identified as female, and 80 percent of the campers were of color. Of the eight teaching fellows, three identified as males, five as females, and were evenly split for racial distribution. The camp was directed by a philosophy faculty member who was a white foreign-born woman; the four invited speakers were all white academics. Lunch, snacks, and transportation as well as a small stipend for attendance were provided to the campers.

The camp was free of charge for campers. Fellows received a stipend and speakers received an honorarium. The university provided the classroom and infrastructure free of charge. It also provided us with administrative assistance. The camp came to be as a result of many people working together, offering their professional and personal support. If a summer camp builds a small world, the persons working to build this world and the persons tending to it bear a special responsibility and merit. It is thanks to many people that our campers came to inhabit and be nourished by this small philosophical world for one week.

TEACHING FELLOWS PREPARATION

The teaching fellows received four days of training in order to develop the pedagogical tools necessary for facilitating philosophy-based discussions and activities. They practiced these tools and techniques in small groups and took turns facilitating different discussions. The adopted pedagogy was loosely modeled after classic Philosophy for Children (P4C) community of inquiry.[2]

Developed in the pragmatist tradition, the pedagogy consists in structuring the group as a community that generates its own questions and shares epistemic responsibility for the quality of the inquiry. The facilitator has the task of setting up the inquiry and monitoring it, making sure that the participants follow agreed-upon rules, and maintaining the quality of the process. The facilitator covers a neutral role that is vital for the philosophical discussion to flow and for participants to take full ownership of their own thinking.

The training that teaching fellows received has proven especially valuable considering that our campers were beginners to the philosophical inquiry, and they needed help learning to take turns and not getting carried away talking more about people rather than ideas. It is important for the facilitator to know when to jump in and steer the conversation back to one of equality of voices and respect for every voice.

Too many times students are exposed to philosophy in a manner that harms their view of what philosophy is, due to ignorance or poor/lack of facilitation. It was crucial for the camp and for our students to make sure that this was not their experience. We wanted to create a safe and friendly environment to introduce and explore philosophy with our campers.[3]

SCHEDULE

A typical day at the camp would run like this: Students began to arrive at a campus classroom at 8:30 a.m. Breakfast snacks were provided, and campers would have conversations among each other and with the teaching fellows. From 9:00 to 10:00 a.m., there would be a warm-up discussion about the topic of the day. This activity was facilitated by a different pair of teaching fellows each day. Next, a guest speaker would give a lecture on the philosophical topic of the day that was intended to simulate a lecture in a typical college course.

The topics of each respective lecture were the questions, "What is philosophy?," "What is learning?," "Is race real?," "Is a river a person?," and "Do computers have minds?" These lectures were followed by a period of open questioning and discussion where campers were encouraged to share their thoughts about the lecture as a full group. The lectures were given by SU faculty and invited lecturers from other schools, with the purpose to expose campers to different styles and genres of philosophy teaching.

The first half of each day would end with small-group writing workshops, led by the teaching fellows. These workshops were focused around developing an understanding of writing conventions to prepare the campers to write their college application essays. Campers shared drafts of their statement of purpose essays with their peers and provided each other with feedback.

The sharing of these personal statements seemed to be a cathartic experience for several of the campers as they revealed some of the harrowing challenges that they faced on their way to becoming prospective college students. Writing the college application essay opened a door to questions of narrative and social identity: this inspired us to choose a theme for the next summer camp 2019: *Philosophy as Self-Knowledge.*

The second half of every day began with lunch at the SU Commons. Students were provided with lunch tickets and were able to have full access to the university's dining hall. Because the philosophical friendships that were starting needed time and tending to in both formal and informal ways, the fellows made sure to sit at the table with the campers and continue the conversations together over lunch.

At around 1:00 p.m., students would leave the dining hall and begin participating in philosophical activity. These activities varied greatly from day to day and included outdoor games and physical activities; the creation of philosophical comic, arts, and crafts such as tie-dyeing a T-shirt; collaborative philosophical games; and a trip to a local ice cream shop. These recreational activities provided students with time to interact and bond with each other in a more relaxed setting. Students would begin being picked up from the camp at 3:00 p.m. Transportation to and from home was provided to campers who needed it and organizing it via a private cab company was probably the most difficult challenge.

GOALS AND PEDAGOGY

The overall goals of the camp were to introduce high school students to philosophy, develop critical thinking skills in a seminar-style environment, and prepare campers for the college application process and enrollment. Students were expected to engage in dialogue with their peers about their respective ideas and questions related to a given topic. This methodology of learning is an inversion of the traditional classroom experience, with which most of the high school students were familiar.

Typically, students are tasked with finding a succinct and correct answer to a question provided by an instructor, but in Socratic inquiry, students are asked to formulate their own questions derived from wherever their sense of wonder may lead them. The result of this inversion allows students to form a meaningful relationship with philosophical ideas by providing them with a level of ownership over the conversation that is not always present in the traditional teaching model. Rather than playing the role of a passive recipient of the information that the instructor espouses, students are active participants in the construction of a free-flowing and educative discussion.

An Example of a Discussion

On the third day of camp, the campers were split into different groups in order to inspect a box. No one could open it because of its tight seal, and only two teaching fellows and one camper knew what was inside. Each group examined the box and the majority made assumptions based on what they heard, saw, and felt. One group mentioned the box needed to be something superlight because they couldn't find a significant shift in weight no matter how it turned. The rest of the students shared their hypotheses: liquid has sound to it, constraints or a limited size, Russian nesting dolls, box inside another box.

To the facilitators' surprise, students were eager to participate and discussed at length what might have seemed a weird question to start with. One camper commented "[that] we didn't know what was in the box connects to the fact that philosophy is undomesticated territory." This expression, "undomesticated territory," was understood as meaning that philosophy is uncharted: compared to other school subjects with clear and discrete answers, philosophical inquiry yields puzzlement and openness.

The students came to a consensus that the item inside the box needed to be superlight. Most of the campers agreed that the mystery item was a piece of paper. The fellows revealed the insides to be some feathers. The box proposed a question of uncertainty and made the campers truly consider a situation from different perspectives. Exercising different methods of thought and forming them around odd situations not usually presented in the daily life can open up new avenues for inquiry. What would make this sound? How much time would I need in order to see if it could be this? Where would I need to hit the box in order to hear a reaction?

Toward the middle of the week, the students realized that their opinions were all valid as long as they were supported by good arguments. A common issue for youth is the shutting down of their ideas because of their age. Good ideas are good ideas, and sometimes younger people can attack issues that have proved to be stagnant to older generations. The campers shared with us these issues and mentioned how relieving they found the opportunity to talk about things without age being an obstacle to being heard or being allowed to contribute.

Often times they would talk about how their teachers talked at them, rather than with them. The distinction they made refers back to the inability to listen to students and vice versa.

Students are unheard or ignored in the typical classroom because children are viewed as being merely unfinished adults. Philosophical conceptions of children as deficient adults can be traced back to Aristotle.[4]

The Aristotelian conception of childhood classifies children as underdeveloped beings who possess the unrealized potential of becoming fully formed adults. When adult teachers apply this Aristotelian "deficient" conception of childhood to students, it should not be surprising to find that those adults are dismissive of the thoughts that their students share with them. In these situations, teachers possess complete intellectual authority, and students are expected to submit to the will of the adult.

Unfortunately, by dismissing the voices of students, the development of their intellectual confidence is impaired. Every time an adult chooses to ignore them, children confirm the belief that their ideas are not worthy of sharing. This problem was addressed at the philosophy camp by placing the pedagogical focus on the thoughts and actions of the campers. The environment the discussion takes place in molds the type of thinking arising from the conversation.

By arranging the room in a circle, at minimum everyone had to hear or face someone who talked and shared their ideas. The format also reduced the power structures that normally exist in a traditional classroom. By having the facilitators scattered around the circle and also engaged in the discussion, the habitual dynamic of teachers talking at their students was altered.

The goal was to create a learning environment where the campers always felt encouraged to participate in discussions because their ideas were held as equally important to those of any adult attending the camp. A romanticized notion of childhood views children as possessing "a form of knowledge no longer accessible to adults,"[5] which means that children's knowledge is considered separate from the kind of knowledge that an adult possesses. It is mysterious to adults who lost the capacity to access children's knowledge and it is considered akin to prophecy, that is, it sounds truthful, divine-like, and incomprehensible to adult logic.

This notion doesn't silence children like the Aristotelian outlook, but it still makes them creatures of adult imagination and doesn't acknowledge them as fully human. Without upholding this romanticized notion of childhood, we wanted to acknowledge younger thinkers as bearing their own knowledge, equally valid and continuous to our world. We wanted to repair the epistemic injustice and stop wronging children as knowers.[6] The world created by the philosophy camp allowed us to achieve our goals and to experience a different model of the relationship between students and teachers.

During the remaining part of the week, the discussions returned to the box activity and the campers referred to it several times: Could we ever have confirmation without opening the box? For some questions, can you ever know the truth? Someone brought up the idea that no one was certain of what was inside the box, therefore no one would know whether or not the inside of it was dangerous. The discussion was abruptly catapulted toward the worth of a risk assessment. The campers began to discuss fragility and the importance of knowing whether or not their examination of the box would bring harm to what was inside.

To some of the campers the boxed truth seemed to be fake, a construction of human thought they believed to be unreliable. One mentioned, "Truth may be more subjective than I had thought before." Another student commented, "There is no such thing as facts." The students were then thinking about the infinity of numbers within numbers and about the reality and objectivity of numbers themselves.

The campers discussed what truth may mean and if we would benefit as a society if truth had more than one definition. As teaching fellows, we decided that no direct answers would be provided by us, but that we would help the campers create and examine their own theories and connect them to the content communicated in that part of the day occupied by the academic lecture.

WHAT IS THE VALUE OF A PHILOSOPHY SUMMER CAMP?

The standard method for raising children follows a particular model of preparing for the real world, in essence they fulfill the role of an inheritor. In a broad sense, children are raised in order to participate successfully within society. As adults, our duty to youth centers on making sure they know the realities of the common world. Therefore, when they start out, children seem to be unaware of the world outside of their immediate familial circle.

A distinction between the world of children and that of the adults exists. Most of the campers mentioned their school experience infantilizes them, by not trusting children with making their own decisions. Philosophy summer camps scaffold a child's ability to function away from home by creating a transitional world in which children can experiment with thinking. Campers discover a sense of themselves as thinkers in relation to others and they learn to value others' voices as well as their own.

Campers benefit from exercising their critical thinking skills and applying those to abstract philosophical ideas or more concrete contemporary issues. The camp emphasized listening carefully to one another, to what the texts say, and to ideas put forward while providing the campers with the space to articulate their thinking. Philosophical discussion resonates with younger groups of people who are skeptical about the world they live in.

It is possible that for youth, the structure of the world does not appear to function as resolutely as adults would lead them to believe. Often times children who attend public school experience a more diverse environment. Thus, in some sense, younger people are primed for philosophical discussion, maybe even more so than adults who are more inclined to believe the world is one set way. It is important for the campers to see the different ways a philosophical conversation can improve their ability to understand those around them in ways not usually afforded by other educational experiences.

It is not always feasible at school to think outside the decided curriculum. Philosophy opened up a space in which campers could think through questions and themes that mattered for them and experience themselves as thoughtful participants in difficult conversations. For example, the campers could engage in inquiries about the environment or the prison system, taking part in dialogues that were relevant and also practical: what we indicate as *tangible conversations*. Toward the end of the camp, the students reflected on their experience and mentioned how much they liked the freedom to think about race, technology, learning, and gender.

A camper mentioned, "It's cool that we get to talk about real stuff and it actually applies to what we see happening in the world." Most of the campers appreciated the space to be allowed to grow both cognitively and emotionally. Teenagers go through a variety of trials with identity and understanding their place in society, experiencing the tensions between the local mentality, which in a small rural center like ours tends to be quite narrow and afraid of newness, and their larger worldly aspirations as they grow toward adulthood.

The students were able to begin forming a conclusion with regard to their respective roles in social groups and the impact they each have as citizens of the world. They were also offered an opportunity to build their confidence by speaking out and having their views listened to, respected, and tested. As we reflect back on the 2018 camp, we look forward to the 2019 summer, hopeful that this new tradition will endure and we will continue creating small philosophical worlds every summer where teenagers, college students, and faculty learn to think together in philosophical friendship.[7]

NOTES

1. SU is a small comprehensive university in the University of Maryland System which serves around 8,000 students. The summer camp was offered in the context of a long-standing collaboration between the Philosophy Department and the Wicomico County Public School System to expand pre-college Philosophy in the local K–12 public schools.

2. See Lipman, Matthew (ed.), 1993, *Thinking Children and Education*, Dubuque, Iowa: Kendall/Hunt; and Lipman, Matthew, Sharp, Ann M., & Oscanyan, Frederick (eds.), 1978, *Growing Up With Philosophy*, Philadelphia: Temple University Press. The P4C pedagogy has become a widely influential philosophy of education practiced worldwide and with a rich and evolving scholarship.

3. Special thanks to Veda Nowowieski, an SU philosophy major and one of the teaching fellows, for her contributions about this section.

4. See Matthews, Gareth, & Mullin, Amy, "The Philosophy of Childhood," The Stanford Encyclopedia of Philosophy (Winter 2018 Edition), Edward N. Zalta (ed.), <https://plato.stanford.edu/archives/win2018/entries/childhood/>.

5. See Kennedy, David, 2006, *The Well of Being: Childhood, Subjectivity, and Education* SUNY series, Early Childhood Education: Inquiries and Insights, p. 45 and following.

6. See Burroughs, M., & Tollefsen, D., 2016. "Learning to Listen: Epistemic Injustice and the Child," *Episteme* 13 (3): 359–377. doi:10.1017/epi.2015.64.

7. The authors are two philosophy majors, Kimberly and Jack, with their undergraduate professor Cristina Cammarano. The whole summer camp and program, as we already mentioned, benefit from the support of a wide net including the Faculty and Staff of the Philosophy Department, and the Fulton School Dean. Renewed thanks to them as well as to the Whiting Foundation for supporting our first Summer Camp 2018.

WORKS CITED

Burroughs, Michael, & Tollefsen, Deborah. (2016). "Learning to Listen: Epistemic Injustice and the Child." *Episteme* 13 (3): 359–377.

Kennedy, David. (2006). *The Well of Being: Childhood, Subjectivity, and Education.* SUNY series, Early Childhood Education: Inquiries and Insights.

Lipman, Matthew, Sharp, Ann M., & Oscanyan, Frederick (eds.). (1978). *Growing Up With Philosophy.* Philadelphia: Temple University Press.

Lipman, Matthew (ed.). (1993). *Thinking Children and Education.* Dubuque, Iowa: Kendall/Hunt.

Matthews, Gareth, & Mullin, Amy. "The Philosophy of Childhood." *The Stanford Encyclopedia of Philosophy* (Winter 2018 Edition), Edward N. Zalta (ed.), <https://plato.stanford.edu/archives/win2018/entries/childhood/>.

Chapter 6

Corrupt the Youth Residential Summer Philosophy Camp

Building a Camp with a Strong Culture

Alex Hargroder and Briana Toole

Corrupt the Youth is a philosophy outreach program that aims to bring philosophy to ethnically and socioeconomically diverse schools in the hopes of making the discipline of philosophy more responsive to and representative of those in the social margins. Corrupt the Youth operates as a chapter-based program that works to create partnerships between Title I schools and local colleges and universities.

In June 2019, Corrupt the Youth offered its first residential summer philosophy camp. We hosted students at the University of Texas at Austin for two weeks, during which time students were enrolled in philosophy classes and participated in residential activities. In this chapter, we will explore how we arrived at the vision for running a camp and the pedagogical approach that emerged as a result, the logistics specific to operating a residential camp on a university campus, as well as brief reflections on fundraising, managing stakeholders, and curriculum design.

Before we discuss how we came to run a two-week residential philosophy camp (while in the middle of a cross-country move!), we should first provide some context for how we ended up on this unlikely and transformative path. When we started Corrupt the Youth, we had a clear sense of what our purpose would be, but not necessarily how we would go about it. We knew we wanted to practice philosophy as an act of resistance against the stifling and disengaging ways that students at the margins experience schooling.

After beginning our careers as public school teachers, starting Corrupt the Youth was by no means a disconnected project, but one that we had harbored in fits and starts throughout our teaching, even when nurturing the critical capacities of students led to backlash from adults who feared that this approach would "disrupt order" and "distract from the curriculum." It occurred to us that this controlling impulse, what Alice Miller (1983) called "poisonous pedagogy," so often directed at students of color and structurally oppressed communities, was neither new nor accidental. And while we knew the scale of this problem was too large to have any one solution, we also saw potential for a community of inquiry driven by philosophical tools and social engagement.

Our vision was to venture beyond this "educational trauma" by putting into practice a liberatory pedagogy in the sense that bell hooks describes in *Teaching to Transgress*, one which works to produce critical thinking facilitated through a culture of trust and deeper learning. With a national trend toward curricula and supervision that narrowly focus on the results of high stakes tests, students often feel mounting frustration and little agency. As a result, many have come to see school as a kind of hazing more than as a process of learning and growth.

Into this, we imagined injecting philosophy, but cast as an opportunity for students to give voice to their curiosities and developing sense of self, while also offering tools and opportunities to engage the critical crosswinds they encountered in their lives. Hence our name, itself a source of minor controversy: we weren't keen to produce a static showpiece or to slot cleanly into existing systems, but instead to carve out and protect a space that could remind students of their critical power and where it can lead.

Our first project was a partnership with a Title 1 high school in East Austin, known locally for its tumultuous history and recent threats of closure by state officials. In our pilot semester in the spring of 2016, we tested the theory of philosophy as a means to social justice, partnering with an academic support elective course. Because a significant component of the course addressed general academic habits and tools for learning, we were able to lead one or two classes each week, in which we would integrate relevant discursive and reflective tools into our vision of a robust, philosophy-informed space where students could explore challenging topics that echoed their own experiences.

Given the relatively generous amount of class time we were afforded, we began to recruit volunteers from the University of Texas's Department of Philosophy to serve as volunteer leaders for each class period. As this process developed, we began to see the potential for an enduring program. While we were able to create an engaging space for students almost immediately, a surprising source of encouragement was the effect we saw on our volunteers from academia. Not only was there an uncommonly strong showing of volunteer support, but also a deeper, less tangible effect that emerged more gradually.

By recasting philosophy to make concepts clear for our adolescent learners, our volunteers engaged students in deep and sustained dialogue regarding issues like gentrification, mass incarceration, and race and gender bias, all of which were rooted in student experience and local contexts. In this way, we hoped to put into practice a pedagogy that reflected our philosophical values—raising the voices of those at the margins—and that is compatible with sustained and careful listening, especially in recognizing the richness of critical contributions that might otherwise be excluded or overlooked.

Briana's experience working at a prestigious academic sleepaway camp for high schoolers helped to inform the early visions of what our camp would become. Seeing the affordances of this fascinating and rarified environment led her to wonder what it might be like to create something like this, but for students who would otherwise be excluded from these prestigious programs because of their social position. Most importantly, it would need to be free for students, so we applied for grants and prizes and more or less left the idea as a thumbnail sketch.

As that idea evolved, the cornerstone of our conceptual design of the camp was that it be "not more school," and instead would be in some ways the inverse of compliance-driven contemporary schooling through an active, democratic, and collaborative culture that focused explicitly on creating a sense of trust with and among campers. Because it was a community rooted in inquiry that we were seeking to build, we aimed to foreground students' experiences and identities as uniquely valuable, and in a more direct sense, employing philosophy as a social practice.

In short, we wanted learning for learning's sake, which we would pursue by guiding extended "conversations" through modeling and allowing space, in class and out, to respond to questions that satisfied this criteria: on the one hand, curiosity directed the path of learning, but on the other, this path was marked by a coherence produced by an overall experience that was bounded by the same basic language and values.

As one of our students wrote in a post-camp reflection, "I think I most appreciated having a dedicated space in which to talk about these subjects, without being told we're 'going off topic' or 'complicating matters unnecessarily.'" We would seek, then, to plan for and then allow moments of flow. We had also decided that we would need to make space to contend with corrosive understandings of schooling, like grades and shame, in order to get closer to reuniting learning with pleasure.

Finally, we wanted to take full advantage of the situated experience on a college campus, by offering the embodied experience of a university's culture and practices, but with an overt focus on how to navigate this space, both practically and emotionally. By creating playful and absorbing experiences that focused on community, we sought to demonstrate the transformative power of a peer group having a shared experience within a developmentally appropriate balance between freedom and supervision (decidedly unlike the schools our campers attended). It is in this sort of environment that students can emerge as their fullest, strongest selves, and thus to access the full range of their abilities.

From here, we will pivot to a more concrete look at the camp's structure and logistics. Our core experience was rooted in students spending their days together in classes, which were led by philosophy graduate student instructors, and evenings would involve residential activities, led by undergraduates who served as residential assistants. Additionally, students spent meals together in dining halls, resided in a dorm, and shared each room with another participant.

These formal and informal settings offered students a chance to connect deeply with each other, as well as to learn about students from different cultural backgrounds and school environments. We had seven staff members, comprising two camp directors, one writing coach, two instructors, and two residential assistants. Of that, two were male and five female. We had four white staff members, two black staff members, and one Hispanic/Latina staff member. Three of our staff (both instructors and one camp director) were graduate students in philosophy. Our two residential assistants were undergraduates enrolled at the University of Texas at Austin.

Prior to arriving at camp, our staff participated in training sessions conducted via the online platform Zoom. We also asked staff to arrive three days prior to the start of camp for in-person training sessions. This was a nice opportunity for us to become more intimately acquainted with each other, as well as with the spaces we would be using for the duration of camp.

While our instructors were in sessions involving pedagogy and project-based design, our residential counselors assembled "swag bags" for our campers (compliments of the American Philosophical Association [APA]) and lanyards for the campers to wear. This last bit is essential. As there may be numerous camps happening simultaneously, having students wear something that immediately identified them as members of our camp was helpful in directing them in spaces they shared with students from other camps.

While we could, as some camps did, choose to have our students dress uniformly (in camp T-shirts, for instance), our goal is to encourage maximum freedom. For our students—many of whom attend tightly regulated schools with an official dress code and uniform—allowing them freedom of dress might seem insignificant, but it was a feature that contributed to the feeling of "not more school" that we were striving for.

Once our staff was in place, the natural next step involved recruiting students for the camp. Marketing ourselves proved to be a distinct challenge. We utilized our collective social and professional networks, making several presentations at local schools, placing a few online advertisements, and creating signage to post at schools citywide. Students were selected based on a few criteria, but our logic in requiring an application was that it would distinguish students who were aligned with our interests and would demonstrate a commitment to following through.

Because this was to be a free camp, we needed strong commitments to ensure that the camp would actually be viable, both in terms of ensuring that students who were selected would show up and in terms of selecting a group that would reflect our mission of bringing critical engagement and rich learning experiences to those who might not otherwise have access to them.

To ensure this, we needed to create a student application that would satisfy three criteria: (1) give us a sense of who would be a good candidate but, (2) not serve a "gatekeeping" function, and (3) give students a sense of what they were getting themselves into, so to speak. Our worry was that an overly pedantic application process would discourage the very students we hoped to serve in offering (and who would most benefit from) a free camp. In the end, we decided on a short application process for students. We asked them to answer two essay prompts—"Why do you want to learn more about philosophy?" and "Describe a time when you learned something new about yourself."—but kept responses to those essays short (250 words maximum per essay).

We later used their answers to the latter prompt during a writing workshop as writing samples that the students could continue to expand upon for college personal statements. This made the applications functional—so that they weren't a waste of time for campers to complete or for us, as staff, to read. We also asked them to rank their top two course preferences. This ensured that they had some sense of what the camp would involve (as they had to read the course descriptions in order to make their determinations), and also helped us as we prepared each student's camp schedule.

We accepted nineteen students into our camp, of which eighteen identified as racial or ethnic minorities, and twelve identified as gender minorities. Ten self-reported that they qualified for free or reduced lunch. Although many of our campers were from the local Austin area, several campers traveled from other areas in Texas. We had one student from Houston and four drove from Brownsville, Texas (a six-hour drive from the U.S.-Mexico border), to participate in the camp. Another three were selected to participate from our New York chapter.

During the camp, we offered four classes in the following subfields: Juries, Judgments, and Justice (Political Philosophy); Who Knows What? Epistemic Injustice, Oppression, and Exploitation (Philosophy of Race and Gender); Trust and Deception (Critical Reasoning); and Why Be Moral? (Ethics). Each camper enrolled in two classes (with all campers taking either political philosophy or critical reasoning). Classes met for three hours in the morning (9:00 a.m.–12:00 p.m.) and the afternoon (1:00 a.m.–4 p.m.), with a thirty-minute break during each class. Students had a one-hour break for lunch and a one-hour break immediately after their afternoon classes (4:00–5 p.m.).

In the evenings, we offered a one-hour writing workshop (5:00–6:00 p.m.) to help students develop personal statements for their college applications. Students had dinner following their writing workshop (6:00–7:00 p.m.), after which they had a two-hour break (from 7:00 to 9:00 p.m.) to participate in a residential activity of their choice (facilitated by our residential assistants). On the Saturday and Sunday that campers were with us, they participated in a three-hour ACT/SAT workshop in the morning (9:00 a.m.–12:00 p.m.) facilitated by the camp directors. The afternoon and evenings were spent in weekend activities led by our RAs.

SAMPLE CAMP SCHEDULE

7:00–9:00 a.m.	Shower and Breakfast
9:00–12:00 p.m.	Class 1
12:00–1:00 p.m.	Lunch
1:00–4:00 p.m.	Class 2
4:00–5:00 p.m.	Free Time
5:00–6:00 p.m.	Writing Workshop
6:00–7:00 p.m.	Dinner
7:00–9:00 p.m.	Residential Activity
9:00–10:00 p.m.	Free time
10:00 p.m.	Lights out

One sign of success in teaching high school-aged students is when they can't give up the learning conversation and it rattles down the hall with them, sometimes for days or longer, because it is now *their* conversation. This was our surest sign that something was working in what we were attempting, even if much of that was still raw and exploratory.

Aside from classes and the philosophical discussions those prompted, residential activities were a highlight for our campers. Each camper was sorted into a group led by one of our RAs. Their RA served as their "camp anchor"—someone they could turn to if they needed guidance or just wanted to talk. Having college students serve in this capacity was excellent, because it gave our campers a chance to talk to someone who had recently been through the college application process.

RA groups also gave the campers a sense of community within the camp. Camp activities planned by the RAs included making flower crowns and dream catchers, water balloon fights, and group hide-and-seek. But, we also wanted RAs to offer opportunities that would allow students to explore the city. Since we had students from as far as New York, as well as some who had traveled from outside Austin, we were keen to show them around the city and campus.

RAs lead tours of the Texas State Capitol building, took students to Barton Springs (a local watering hole), played laser tag, and explored events hosted by the city (like Music in the Park and Blues on the Green). Students also enjoyed the on-campus bowling alley, participating in many spirited matches of air hockey; they attended an open mic night at UT's infamous Cactus Cafe; and they enjoyed the beautiful athletic facilities of Gregory gymnasium. As one of our Austin students marveled, it was a great opportunity to "see my home through another's eyes." For our students from New York, simple things, like driving through the city, provided a radically different version of city life.

Camp thus served a dual role. The goal was not only to provide an opportunity for students to explore philosophy but also to demystify the college experience. Many of our students reported feeling much more confident about the aspect of applying to and attending college after the camp than they had before. In part, this is because for many of our students, they lack financial opportunities to participate in home away camps. Consequently, they struggle to imagine what it will be like to leave home and start over again in a new environment.

The residential camp helped them explore what opportunities are available for community-building on college campuses, as well as what resources (gyms, writing centers, health centers, etc.) are available on college campuses. It gave them an opportunity to see what it is like to live in a dorm, to eat meals on campus, to make new friends, and to explore new places.

It also offered them a sense of independence and the opportunity to explore who they are away from their families and existing community and group of friends. As one parent wrote reflecting on her child's experience, "She had a feeling of independence and a little taste of what college life could be like." In short, participation in a residential camp gave our students a basis for which to imagine their own college life. This is especially so for students of parents who may not have attended college and so cannot offer insight into the experience.

On this note, it is helpful to think about potential challenges involving your camp stakeholders. Stakeholders might include donors, the university or department hosting the camp, your staff, parents, and students (to name but a few). We found our biggest challenge to be parents, many of whom were wary of the camp for many reasons.

Some parents found a free camp suspicious, and many worried it might be a scam. Moreover, as we prioritized low-income students who might not have had an opportunity to attend a residential camp, we were targeting students who were unlikely to have been away from their parents for extended periods of time. Many of our parents found the idea of leaving their children with relative strangers somewhat unnerving. For some of our students who came from an all-girls school, their parents were nervous about the coeducational aspect of the camp. We did as much as we could to alleviate concerns that parents might have in this regard.

The camp director (Briana) called all parents to speak with them about the camp, to provide arrival and departure information, and to collect information regarding their child's necessary medications, emergency contact information, and so on. We found that speaking to parents directly, answering any questions they had regarding the logistics of the camp, and making sure they had my contact information put most parents at ease. Even so, we found that parents were anxious when they were dropping their children off. We did several things that we believe helped in this respect.

First, we had student groups at UT offer the parents a campus tour, which put them at ease since it gave them a better sense of the physical environment their children would be in. Second, following the campus tour, our camp director offered a welcome session to the parents and their children, explaining why we were offering the camp and how we were able to offer it for free (and sharing how much the camp would have cost were it *not* free). More than putting the parents at ease, this invested them heavily in our program, because it gave them a more thorough understanding both of Corrupt the Youth's mission and of the motivations of the people to whom they were entrusting their children.

Finally, at the conclusion of camp, we held one-on-one meetings with each parent and their child to review (1) what their child had done at camp, (2) areas of strength and growth for their child, and (3) a college preparation packet, complete with information about applying for colleges, scholarships, and financial aid. This demonstrated to parents that we were invested in their children and committed to helping them succeed.

Many parents followed up with us to express their gratitude for the program and to report positive changes they had seen in their child following camp. As one parent wrote about their son in the end-of-camp parent survey, "He in fact came back more excited about the college life and continuing his education. What I did not expect was for him to tell me that this has been the best experience of his life and I was happy to hear that."

Aside from worries that parents may have, one of the most difficult aspects of a residential camp involves securing funding. For a residential camp, you should anticipate the following costs: dormitories for students and staff; on-campus meals for students and staff, as well as snacks for students throughout the day; supplies for residential activities and any costs associated with events; transportation and parking; health insurance; as well as salaries or stipends for your staff. Altogether, the 2019 Summer Camp cost approximately $28,000.

We were fortunate to secure funding through a combination of means, though primarily we were funded by two large grants: one from the APA ($20,000) and one from the Philosophy Learning and Teaching Organization ($5,660). We were also aided in part by the philosophy department at the University of Texas, with the provision of a $1,500 grant from their Bob Solomon fund. The remaining funds were from individual donors.

Residential camps are difficult and expensive to plan and operate. Here we have not sought to provide a guide for how to implement your own camp, but a reflection on our own experience of arriving at the idea to offer a camp. There are, of course, important logistical points to think through as you plan your own camp. But it is more important to ask yourself what you hope to accomplish in doing so. Do you want students to emerge as more critical thinkers? Do you want them to feel more familiar in a college environment? Do you hope to help them develop a better understanding of their world?

The only way to have the energy and commitment to put together a good camp is to have a vision that is strong enough to keep you going. Otherwise, you are just teaching philosophy to kids in the summer. And that is just more school.

Chapter 7

From the Ground Up
Developing a High School Philosophy Camp
Charlie Kurth and Adam Waggoner

High school students want to do philosophy. They want to think about "big questions." They want to get better at developing and defending their ideas. These are all things that philosophy summer camps can do—and do well. While interest in developing these camps is growing, the supply is far short of the demand. In Michigan, for instance, the 2019 Western Michigan Lyceum in Kalamazoo drew students from the Northern Indiana and the Detroit suburbs—each over two hours away!

This guide is meant to both help philosophy departments understand the value and rewards of developing a philosophy summer camp, and lay out the nuts and bolts of putting a camp together. The discussion that follows is inspired by the Western Michigan Lyceum, a weeklong philosophy summer camp for high school students facilitated primarily by the graduate students in the Western Michigan University Philosophy MA program. The Lyceum is entering its fourth year of operation. In this time, the number of campers attending has more than doubled, the students now come from a more diverse range of schools, and the project has gained the attention of both the WMU administration and the Kalamazoo community more generally.

WHY RUN A HIGH SCHOOL PHILOSOPHY SUMMER CAMP?

By participating in philosophy summer camps, high school students are exposed to philosophy in a fun, engaging, and supportive environment. Along with honing participants' critical thinking skills, philosophy summer camps tend to draw in high school students interested in discussing "big questions" with their peers: What does it mean to be a person? How can I know anything? What does a just society look like? Exploring questions like these often leads to exciting new friendships forged by students across a range of grade levels, schools, convictions, and socioeconomic backgrounds.

The opportunity to engage with one another and the camp leaders in a college setting also tends to leave students more comfortable discussing their views with others, helps them identify problems with their own views and the views of those around them, and increases their college readiness. These benefits are recognized not only by camp leaders and parents but by the high school students themselves. Consider, for instance, the remarks from a Lyceum participant:

> The Lyceum cultivates an environment of friendship, casual learning, and respect for one another's ideas that is not present in a typical high school classroom. Students are encouraged to speak their minds, to take a stance, to seek answers, and to question others. I have learned to create and present a strong argument, but also to listen to others and to change my mind. I have met some really incredible and interesting people through this summer camp, and I would absolutely recommend the Lyceum to anyone interested in Philosophy, in exciting discussions, or in thinking about the world.

Philosophy summer camps are also an enriching experience for the camp leaders, whether they be faculty members, graduate students, or undergraduate students. Working with high school students in an environment less formal than a classroom often rekindles a passion for both teaching and studying philosophy among camp leaders. It can also prompt camp leaders to facilitate philosophical conversation in new, innovative ways. As one recent WMU Lyceum leaders notes,

> In my first year of grad school, I was feeling a little burnt out with respect to philosophy. Participating in the Lyceum really recharged my batteries, though. The Lyceum is an environment where there is more fun to be had doing philosophy. And it is also a kind of workshop space for those instructing or delivering any content. It is a really interesting challenge to deliver accurate and quality content on these subjects in a way that is accessible and engaging for the high school

audience. My overall experience with the Lyceum has been wholly positive, a great growth experience, and a ton of fun.

Finally, a philosophy summer camp is advantageous to both the department that supports the program and the respective college or university: high school students—and their parents—gain a close, hopefully positive, connection to the camp leaders, the campus, and the department that is running the camp. Such positive connections increase the likelihood of high school students attending the host college and taking classes, or even majoring, in philosophy. For instance, one of last year's campers is now enrolled at WMU. As she explained in her exit survey, the Lyceum "was a huge factor in my decision to major in philosophy."

WHAT RESOURCES ARE REQUIRED TO RUN A PHILOSOPHY SUMMER CAMP WELL?

An answer to this question largely depends on the size and scope of the camp in question. For example, a smaller philosophy summer camp can flourish with only a few camp leaders, while a larger camp is difficult to facilitate without more support. Thus, running a philosophy summer camp requires a sense of how many students and faculty are willing to participate in the camp before planning recruitment strategies.

Despite the major differences across philosophy summer camps, a core group of undergraduate or graduate students willing to plan and attend the camp, as well as some departmental or institutional support, is vital for almost any camp's continued success. And while such support may take a variety of forms, it is ideal to have at least one faculty adviser who serves as a bridge between students and administrators, helps students plan curriculum, and establishes the program's reputation among prospective parents and local schools.

As an example, the 2019 WMU Lyceum had a core group of three individuals who did the bulk of the recruiting, organization, and lesson plan design. For the camp itself, the typical session had about a 3:1 student-to-facilitator ratio. This low ratio fosters opportunities for participants to form close relationships with camp leaders, inviting conversations about their college and career plans, as well as the various, nonphilosophical activities they enjoy. The hour lunch sessions—where graduate students, faculty, and high school participants eat together—have been a particularly effective venue for these conversations.

The WMU Lyceum costs approximately $50 to $75 per student to run, with the central costs including background checks for graduate student facilitators, a food budget (e.g., snacks and lunch to campers and instructors, refreshments for the concluding research presentation), field trip expenses (e.g., admission, transportation), and a budget to provide each camper with a philosophy book aimed at an issue they have shown interest in over the course of the camp.

At the Lyceum, the lunch and book costs are the largest expenses. But they are also the most important ones. The lunches allow students and instructors to continue conversations from the morning sessions, thus providing an important avenue for further, but more casual, philosophical conversation. Giving each student a book that is selected based on their individual philosophical interests promotes continued interest in philosophy. Lyceum attendees have mentioned both the lunches and the books as highlights of their experiences at the camp.

HOW SHOULD A PHILOSOPHY SUMMER CAMP BE PLANNED?

The following is based on a rough time line for the 2019 WMU Lyceum and its planning, revised to reflect what did and did not work in the first three years. This time line is meant for those looking to start a program from the ground up but will hopefully also provide insights for those who have already started a camp.

In early to mid-fall, the camp's core leaders should hold a meeting to see how many students and faculty are interested in participating in the philosophy summer camp. Here are some key questions to consider: Will the camp have a theme? If so, what will it be? When will the camp take place? What leadership roles are important, and who will occupy them? What costs will the camp have (books? food? field trip?)? Should the camp have a small tuition fee paid by the campers or will be it funded in some other way (e.g., grants, department funds, or college outreach moneys)?

Even as early as the fall, camp planners should begin brainstorming ways to advertise the camp to high school students. Getting the word out is crucial.

If there are local high school ethics bowl or debate teams, this is a great place to start. Moreover, it is important to both establish relationships with high school principals and teachers, and take advantage of already existing connections that the college/university may have with local schools. It is also important to check with college/university administrators about the need for background checks for camp instructors, official college/university approval for the camp, and other administrative or legal requirements.

At this point, it will also be helpful to begin researching funding opportunities. In addition to seeking funds from the university's philosophy department and other college/university bodies (e.g., dean's office, research and community outreach centers), it is also good to contact the institution's student government association, which may offer funding for students to pursue summer camp programming. External grants from philosophical organizations and local community foundations offer other potential sources of funding.

By the end of the fall semester, finalize the camp's date and theme, any potential field trips, and the camp's location. As the winter break approaches, discuss promotional materials and recruitment strategy for the spring semester. When classes resume, promotional materials, such as a camp website, posters, and official registration with the college or university, can be finalized. These promotional materials should be distributed to local high schools, community organizations, and intercampus resources. Approximately one month before classes end, it is good to finalize camp leaders and begin planning curriculum (see the next section for an example).

HOW SHOULD A PHILOSOPHY SUMMER CAMP BE TAUGHT?

The following curriculum is based on the 2019 WMU Lyceum, the theme of which was Philosophy and Technology. Note that this is only a rough skeleton for the camp. Each day's sessions should remain flexible, taking advantage of occasions where fruitful conversations develop among students organically. Thus, it is helpful for camp leaders to meet throughout the week and find ways to mold the curriculum around student interests. While the content and style of the WMU Lyceum sessions varied quite a bit by topic and facilitator, both camp leaders and student participants reported that problem-based, group-oriented, active learning was better than lecture-based learning.

For example, rather than camp leaders explaining the difficulties faced by various theories of personal identity, they might instead facilitate a brainstorming session among participants on what makes them the individuals they are. From here, the camp leaders can then split participants into groups and work with them to engage in a debate. Activities like these help keep philosophical issues interesting, encourage each participant's involvement, and further the camp's goal of introducing student to philosophy in a fun, engaging manner.

Sample Schedule

	Tuesday	Wednesday	Thursday	Friday	Saturday
10–11 a.m.	Logic	Logic	Logic	Field Trip Follow-up	Research Presentations (Parents Invited)
11 a.m.– noon	Metaphysics and Epistemology	Metaphysics and Epistemology	Metaphysics and Epistemology	Research for Final Presentation	
Noon– 1 p.m.	Lunch	Lunch	Lunch	Lunch	
1–3 p.m.	Ethics	Campus Tour	Brains, Minds, and AI	Ethics of Self-driving Cars	
3–5 p.m.	Censorship and Social Media	Research for Final Presentation	Field Trip: Virtual Reality Lab	Student Choice and Send-off	

FOLLOW THROUGH: SURVEYS AND PUBLICITY

The continued success of the camp turns on learning about what went well and what did not. It also benefits from buy-in from one's college/university and community. The WMU Lyceum solicits feedback in variety of ways: exit surveys asking campers to rate various aspects of their experience, surveys soliciting testimonials and input from instructors about the camp's effectiveness, and e-mailed satisfaction inquiries to parents.

On the camper feedback forms, some questions are content-oriented and can be used to identify ways to improve the camp (e.g., What parts of the camp did you find most/least enjoyable?). Other questions are geared toward the overall outcomes of the camp (e.g., rate how much you feel the camp improved your critical thinking skills, improved your confidence in defending your views, grew your interest in studying philosophy). Responses to questions like these can be useful for tracking the overall effectiveness of the camp with regard to its learning outcomes. They also provide data that can be used in grant applications and fundraising efforts.

A further benefit of information gathered from these sources is that it can be used to highlight the camp's success. For instance, it can be used in e-mails and newsletters sent to students, faculty, alumni, and administrators. It can also be sent to local newspapers, high school principals, and community organizations. Through efforts like these, the WMU Philosophy Department now not only sponsors the Lyceum but also sponsors a philosophy club at a local high school.

Part II

SAMPLE ACTIVITIES AND LESSON PLANS

Chapter 8

Lesson Plan

Justice and Different Types of Evidence

James Fritz

MATERIALS

Scripts
Questions to guide discussion
Chairs set up to mimic a courtroom
Optional: costumes (e.g., gavel, robes, or wig)

LESSON PLAN

- Assign roles: We need twelve people to be jurors for both trials, and of the remaining eight-ish people, we need actors. For each trial, we will need a judge, a prosecuting attorney, a defending attorney, and a defendant.
- Briefly explain to students the shape of the exercise: we will play out a courtroom trial, and then the jury will have to deliberate in an adjoining room about whether to find the defendant guilty or not guilty.
    - The standard to aim for is that the defendant must be proven guilty "beyond a reasonable doubt," although there is not much clarity about what that means. So we should just aim to rule in the way that we think would be most *just*.
    - If, after fifteen minutes of deliberation, there is no unanimous verdict, then we will have a hung jury and a mistrial.
- Trial 1: Have students (or instructors, if students are too shy to volunteer) read through the first trial. Ham it up as far as possible!

- After the trial, the twelve jurors are dismissed into an adjoining room. But all instructors, and the eight actor students, follow them and sit around the edge of the room, taking notes on which points seem particularly good for the discussion to follow.
- Allow up to fifteen minutes for discussion—although that is hopefully considerably less than necessary. Students will likely find the defendant guilty very quickly.
* Same drill for Trial 2: again, students will likely reach a verdict more quickly, though they are more likely to go for not guilty.
* Bring everyone together for a discussion. Include the following questions to motivate discussion:
  - What were some of the most persuasive arguments in favor of treating these two cases differently?
    * Are there any powerful responses to those arguments? (For instance, if people say that we get information that is just about a group that the person belongs to in case 2, can't we recast the information that we get in case 1 to also reflect what group the person belongs to? S/he belongs to the group of people who are generally identified on footage of theft and who have stolen goods in their houses.)
  - What were some of the most persuasive arguments in favor of treating the two cases the same way?
    * Are there any powerful responses to those arguments? (For instance, if people say that it is all just about probability, can we problematize the relevant notion of probability?)
  - What are some good general rules to follow about when it is just to convict someone and when it is not?
  - Do the numbers matter here—if the number was 1 in 1,000 instead of 1 in 500, would you treat either case differently? Or 1 in 10,000?
  - Does the seriousness of the crime matter? If the person in the first case was charged with murder, not just petty larceny, would it be more or less attractive to convict him/her? If the prison riot had turned deadly, would it be more or less attractive to convict solely on the basis of percentage of prisoners who participated?
  - Are there good reasons for adopting or for denying an extreme view, like "no one should ever be convicted of a crime," or "it is never against justice to convict someone of a crime as long as she belongs to some reference class that is more than 50 percent criminals?"
  - The problem at hand here resembles a more general problem: Can we ever justify believing a person has some trait solely because they belong to a group in which that trait is very common? If not, why not?

- Closure: "There are serious puzzles about just when we have enough evidence to justly convict a person. We have talked a lot about one of the most immediately attractive positions, which is that you should convict whenever your evidence makes guilt probable to a certain degree. But this position is tough to maintain when you get pairs of cases like the one we saw today: in each, the defendant has the same probability of being guilty. Keep thinking more about this—it is an area in which a lot of people are doing current philosophical work!"

Appendix: Scripts for the two courtroom scenes.

TRIAL #1

Characters

Judge
Prosecuting attorney
Defending attorney
Defendant: Mr./Ms. Graham

Script

Judge: This court is called to session. The defendant, Mr./Ms. Graham, stands accused of stealing a flat-screen TV from target, which carries a charge of petty larceny. This charge carries a sentence that could involve fines up to $1,000. Let us begin the trial.
Prosecuting attorney: Your honor, we call the defendant, Mr./Ms. Graham, to the stand.
  (Mr./Ms. Graham takes the stand.)
Prosecuting attorney: Mr./Ms. Graham, are you aware that video surveillance footage of the theft in question has been found?
Defendant: Yes, I am.
Prosecuting attorney: Are you aware that you were identified in that footage?
Defendant: No, that is impossible, because I didn't commit the crime.
Prosecuting attorney: I will rephrase the question. Are you aware that everyone who has seen the footage, other than you and your parents, has positively identified you as the person stealing the TV?
Defendant: Everyone else must have it out for me, or something! I don't know why they would say that!

Prosecuting attorney: And are you aware that the stolen TV was found in your garage?

Defendant: Yes, but I have no idea how it got there! Someone must have planted it there.

Prosecuting attorney: And can you explain where you were on the night that the TV was stolen?

Defendant: I was at home by myself, reading.

Prosecuting attorney: But you can't provide any evidence for that alibi, or corroborate it with anyone else's testimony?

Defendant: No.

Prosecuting attorney: No further questions, your honor.

Defending attorney: I have a few questions for the defendant, your honor.

Judge: Proceed.

Defending attorney: Mr./Ms. Graham, do you think it is possible that someone can be misidentified on video surveillance footage, even by an enormous amount of people?

Defendant: I guess it is got to be possible, because it is happening!

Defending attorney: But you are not sure just how frequently it happens that, say, more than fifty people all misidentify the person in surveillance footage?

Defendant: No, I am not

Defending attorney: And do you know how often stolen items are stored in the garage of a person who is innocent?

Defendant: No.

Defending attorney: Well, I can help you with both those questions. Allow me to submit into evidence an academic study about evidence for theft. It looked at 500 cases in which everyone agreed that a suspect was identified by video surveillance footage, and the stolen items were found at that suspect's house. The study shows that, when both of these factors come together, the suspect is almost always guilty. But there was one case out of the 500 in which, even though the person appeared to be on surveillance footage and the stolen items were found at her house, she was innocent! She had been cleverly framed. So, my question is, "Could that have also happened in this case?"

Defendant: That must be what happened, because I didn't steal the TV.

Defending attorney: Members of the jury, I plead you, find my client not guilty. Yes, surveillance footage does appear to show him/her stealing a TV. And yes, the TV was found at his house. But, in at least one out of 500 studied cases that are just like this one, all that evidence was misleading because the person was framed. So there is a possibility that all the evidence against my client might be misleading too.

Judge: Members of the jury, it is now your job to reach a unanimous verdict: Do you find this defendant guilty or not guilty? If you judge that the defendant is guilty beyond a reasonable doubt, you must convict.

TRIAL #2

Characters

Judge
Prosecuting attorney
Defending attorney
Defendant: Mr./Ms. Carter

Script

Judge: This court is called to session. The defendant, Mr./Ms. Carter, is already serving a prison sentence. S/he stands accused of participating in a prison riot that seriously hurt several guards. If s/he is convicted, s/he will have to serve six extra months at the end of his/her prison sentence.
Prosecuting attorney: Your honor, we call the defendant, Mr./Ms. Carter, to the stand.
(Mr./Ms. Carter takes the stand.)
Prosecuting attorney: Mr./Ms. Carter, are you aware of the number of prisoners that participated in the riot last week?
Defendant: I heard there were 499 people who were involved in the riot.
Prosecuting attorney: And how many people are housed at the prison?
Defendant: Five hundred.
Prosecuting attorney: Five hundred! So, out of those 500 people, every single prisoner except one participated in the riot.
Defendant: Yep, everyone except me.
Prosecuting attorney: So you are asking us to believe that you are the single prisoner who didn't participate in the prison riots?
Defendant: Yes, because it is the truth!
Prosecuting attorney: Do you have any evidence that you didn't choose to participate in the riot?
Defendant: No, but I shouldn't have to have any evidence that I didn't riot—I am innocent until proven guilty!
Prosecuting attorney: But isn't there an awfully high likelihood that you *are* guilty? You have just admitted that 499 out of 500 prisoners rioted. So, from the jury's perspective, isn't there a 99.8 percent chance that you rioted? And isn't that enough to prove—with only a tiny, tiny, 0.2 percent chance—that you were involved?
Defendant: That is crazy! You can't say you have proven that I acted a certain way just because a lot of other people like me acted that way.
Prosecuting attorney: I have no further questions, your honor.
Defending attorney: I have a few questions for the defendant, your honor.
Judge: Proceed.

Defending attorney: Mr./Ms. Carter, has anyone suggested to you that there is any evidence that you specifically were one of the people who chose to riot?

Defendant: No, the only evidence they have is this statistic that 499 people out of 500 rioted.

Defending attorney: So they don't have any evidence that suggests you were in the group of 499 instead of the group of 1? They are just relying on the high likelihood that you were in the group of 499 to power their entire case?

Defendant: That seems like exactly what they are doing.

Defending attorney: Well, that sounds simply unjust to me. Jury members, I implore you to find my defendant innocent. To convict her based solely on the fact that she is housed at a very statistically unruly prison is nothing more than ruthless stereotyping.

Judge: Members of the jury, it is now your job to reach a unanimous verdict: Do you find this defendant guilty or not guilty? If you judge that the defendant is guilty beyond a reasonable doubt, you must convict.

Chapter 9

Lesson Plan

How Should Scientists Choose the Best Theory?

Roger Sansom

Science is our best way to discover things about the natural world and considers its greatest discoveries to be general theories or laws. For example, Newton's law of gravity states that all objects are attracted to every other object, and strength of that attraction depends on the mass of the objects and the distance between them. Not only does it apply to every object of mass anywhere in the universe today, but it also applies all the way into the past and future. Of course, scientists cannot observe every object and every time to test whether each object follows the law of gravity, so how should they decide to accept such a bold claim?

One answer is to observe a bunch of objects and, if they all follow the law of gravity, conclude that all of the other ones do too. But this comes with a risk of getting things wrong. For example, every swan that European scientists had seen before 1697 was white, so they thought all swans were white. But then the Dutch explorer Willem de Vlamingh reported black swans in Australia. So how can we be sure about our general laws if we cannot observe everything? Philosophers of science have worried about this problem for a long time. They wondered how many observations of what sort were enough that it became reasonable to conclude that the law was true, or at least probably true (this is called *the problem of induction*).

Karl Popper is a twentieth-century philosopher of science who thought that this problem was unsolvable. There was no number or type of observations that we could make to have good reason to believe that a theory was even probably true. What's more, this problem was so serious that it required us to rethink how we understand and practice science.

Popper encouraged scientists to give up on the idea that they should try to prove that scientific laws were true. Instead, they should try to prove them false. The logic goes like this. If all objects are supposed to be attracted to each other by gravity, and we observe one that is not, then we can know that the law is false. If, on the other hand, the object does what the law says it is supposed to do, we do not prove the law true, we just fail to prove it false. If we make many such observations, we may say that the law has often passed tests, but that does not mean that it is true.

This view of science widely influenced scientists and educators. This lesson plan puts students in the place of scientists to see how observations from experiments or other investigations should impact how we should choose our theories. Hopefully, they will learn that although evidence is crucial to science, the way that it should be used is not nearly as simple as Popper believed, and may be quite mysterious.

THEORIZING ABOUT PHLOGISTON

This lesson plan is ideal for classrooms with around 25 students, but it can also be extended to around 100. Arrange the class into groups of between four and six people. Sections in quotes are suggestions of things to say.

"Our first exercises will give you the chance to think like scientists did hundreds of years ago."

"Science is our best way of learning about the world. Science is focused on general theories, and has rejected theories that it once thought were true. One of these rejected theories is the phlogiston theory of combustion. According to this theory of combustion there was an invisible substance with no smell called phlogiston. Combustion (i.e., fire) was the release of phlogiston from the fuel into the air."

"The year is 1770. We are all leading chemistry research groups of our time. As world experts on chemistry, we believe what most 1770 scientists believe: namely, that fire is the release of phlogiston. Some other people think that fire is the absorption of oxygen, but we are pretty sure that they are wrong."

(Just to check that everyone understands what is going on, ask the class.)

"Let us start with something basic. Knowing that fire is the release of phlogiston, why do some things like wood and coal burn so well and something like water does not burn at all?"

(The answer everyone should be able to give is that some things contain lots of phlogiston and some contain none at all.)

"Welcome to the 1770 Chemistry Association annual general meeting. Our objective is to resolve 'the vacuum problem.' Given that combustion is the release of phlogiston, why is it that fire will not burn in a vacuum? Specifically, if we light a candle in a sealed jar and use a pump to suck out the air, the fire quickly goes out. In your research groups, figure out an explanation of this phenomenon that is consistent with phlogiston theory. Understand that answers that sound like oxygen theory, according to which combustion is the absorption of oxygen from the air, will not be well-received."

(You may choose to ham this up by saying that oxygen theory is being advocated by Laurent Lavoisier, who is the tax collector for the French king. He is not a sympathetic character. The French certainly did not think so when they sent him to the guillotine in 1794!) (figure 9.1).

The students need time to figure out how to solve this challenge. Usually around ten minutes is enough. They may decide that phlogiston needs a medium to hold it and if there is no air, it cannot leave the wax currently

The vacuum problem.

1) Fuel does not burn in a vacuum.

Figure 9.1 The Vacuum Problem.

holding it. Maybe it needs something from the air to push it out of the wax. That sounds a bit like oxygen theory but maybe okay. Most likely, most groups will do a fairly good job of coming up with something plausible.

After ten minutes or so, ask each group if they have a solution. If only one group comes up with an idea, share it with the rest of the class so they can see what a solution sounds like and then tell them that they need to come up with a different one.

When every group has its solution, it is time for them to report them to class. Now, they are the experts and you are helping them facilitate their explanation to the class. You can draw it on the board or let them do it as they explain.

After each group has explained their solution, ask the rest of the conference what they think of it. Probably, some explanations will be effectively just like another group's, which is just fine—great minds think alike. Others may be different, but still plausible. Still others might have some sort of problems. For example, if the phlogiston is released from the candle to be attached to the air, why is it not then released from the air, causing the air to catch fire?

If the problem is not itself confused, an explanation may need to be supplemented or changed, or even rejected altogether. That is okay. The conference is not expected to all agree on the same solution, but each solution must be good enough to be found to be plausible by the conference.

(Below is an optional extra conference with a problem to solve. If you judge that you have more than enough time to get through everything else here, the 1771 conference can be included, otherwise skip to 1772.) (figure 9.2).

"Welcome to the 1771 Chemistry Association annual general meeting. Having solved the 'vacuum problem,' we now face a new phenomenon to be explained by phlogiston theory, the 'air volume problem.' Air decreases in volume during combustion. Specifically, consider a glass jar that air can only enter by going through a long narrow vertical glass tube, but it is sealed by a drop of oil. If we burn a candle in the jar, initially the drop rises as the air is heated. However, after the fire is out and everything returns to room temperature, the drop of oil is lower than it was at the beginning of the experiment. The amount of space being taken up by the air has been reduced. This is surprising given that combustion is the release of phlogiston into the air."

Repeat the process of groups coming up with a solution and reporting them back to the conference. Some groups may propose something that fits with

The air volume problem.

2) The volume of air decreases during combustion.

Figure 9.2 The Air Volume Problem.

their explanation for their solution to the vacuum problem, but others may have to develop an explanation that does not fit. When the explanations are being assessed, everyone should be checking that their view of combustion can account for the vacuum problem too.

"Welcome to the 1772 Chemistry Association annual general meeting. Having solved the 'vacuum problem' and 'air volume problem,' we now face a new phenomenon to be explained by phlogiston theory, the 'fuel mass problem' (see figure 9.3). Some fuels get heavier when they are burned. Specifically, if we weigh a piece of sulfur or phosphorus, then burn it, let it cool, and weigh it again, we find that it gets heavier." (Lavoisier discovered this in 1772.)

Repeat the process of groups coming up with a solution and reporting them back to the conference. Not only is this a hard problem, but any solution must solve all three problems. Some groups may not be able to come up with anything, but probably most groups will. Some may borrow ideas from other groups which is okay. Scientists use each other's ideas all the time. Faced with this problem, phlogiston theorists proposed that phlogiston had negative mass. Is that incoherent or should we allow it? You may face exactly this question or something similarly weird. How weird is so weird that it makes an explanation completely implausible?

The fuel mass problem.

3) Certain metals gain mass during combustion (e.g. sulfur and phosphorous).

Time 1   Time 2

Figure 9.3 The Fuel Mass Problem.

The purpose of the above exercises was to show that scientists can accommodate observations that appear to prove a theory false. In fact, scientists routinely do exactly that. The theories typically do not change, but additional facts about what is going on are proposed, such as there is another planet, or phlogiston needs to attach to air particles and reconfigure them to take up less space. The exercise below deals with the implications of the lesson from the previous exercise.

PHILOSOPHY OF THEORY CHOICE

"It is no longer the 1870s and you are no longer world-class scientists; you are world-class philosophers of science. We face a problem."

"Science likes to discover general theories or laws. For example, Newton's law of gravity states that all objects are attracted to every other object. This applies to every object of mass anywhere in the universe today—past, present, and future. Scientists cannot observe every object and every time to test whether each object follows the law of gravity. Additionally, you have just demonstrated that scientists cannot disprove a theory simply by making an observation that initially looked like it contradicted a theory.

Fuels gaining mass when they burn did not simply prove phlogiston theory wrong, because you demonstrated that phlogiston theory could explain the increase in mass of fuels during combustion. And this is not always the wrong thing to do. Scientists routinely discover ways to keep established theories despite problematic evidence. For example, Uranus wasn't moving how it was supposed to according to the law of gravity, so proposed that there must be another planet whose gravity was moving it, and that is how Neptune was discovered. So, when should you keep the old theory and when should you accept a different one?"

"Evidence is crucial to science, but the way that it influences theory choice has puzzled philosophers of science for over 100 years. In the rest of this class, you will propose solutions to the problem."

"Consider oxygen theory's explanation of the phenomena that were problems for phlogiston theory.

The vacuum problem. Fire does not burn in a vacuum because there is no oxygen gas available to be absorbed by the fuel.

The air volume problem. The volume of the air is reduced during combustion because oxygen changes from being a gas in the air (where it takes up lots of space) to being a solid on the surface of the fuel (where it takes up less space).

The fuel mass problem. The mass of fuel can increase during combustion because it is acquiring oxygen from the air.

In your groups, compare these explanations to your group's phlogiston explanations. Which is better?"

This should not take long. You can expect each of the groups to decide that they think oxygen theory does provide better explanations. Below is the final exercise for groups who come to that conclusion and below are exercises for any groups who do not come to that conclusion. In each case, after groups have carried out the exercise they can report back to the class and answers can be compared.

For groups who decide that oxygen theory's explanations are better.

"What are the features of better explanations that indicate that we should choose their theory? History tells us that science preferred oxygen theory's explanations to phlogiston theory's explanations of these phenomena. Your job is to justify this historical choice and look for what it tells us about future choices between theories that we may have to make."

For groups who decide that phlogiston theory's explanations are better.

"What are the features of better explanations that indicate that we should choose their theory? History tells us that science preferred oxygen theory's explanations to phlogiston theory's explanations of these phenomena.

Your job is to show why this historical choice was wrong and look for what it tells us about future choices between theories that we may have to make."

If they decide that they are equally good . . .

"Will explanations for rival theories always be equally good for all phenomena? If so, then science cannot choose between theories based on which one gives the best explanations. If that is the case, then how can scientists choose between theories? Does it matter if they cannot?"

FURTHER ISSUES

This lesson plan deals with a problem that philosophers of science call *the underdetermination of theory choice*. It has been the central problem for philosophy of science for over fifty years. Most philosophers judge that science has usually chosen its theories well given the evidence of the time, but exactly how it does this is complicated.

Radical philosophers (such as Thomas Kuhn, in *The Structure of Scientific Revolution*) have claimed that theory choice is a matter of convention, politics, aesthetics, and so on. The problem for this view is that it does not seem consistent with the way that we use our successful theories. We use them to engineer how we interact with the world. We produce medicine to kill viruses, rather than bleed people to reduce their black bile, and we build combustion engines based on oxygen theory, rather than phlogiston. The theories we choose appear to make a difference in our success in these endeavors and we think that, on the whole, we have chosen wisely.

Two curious phenomena remain. First, sometimes bias has influenced science. For example, in the Soviet Union, Mendelian genetics and evolution by natural selection were rejected in favor of Lamarkianism for reasons of politics. Mendelianism meant that people were born different, which did not fit as well with communist ideology. This did not last forever, but it shows that politics can interfere with science and raises the question of whether we might be under a different bias of some sort.

Second, science has repeatedly chosen a theory that it later rejects. It would be nice to say that it has chosen the least bad theory that had been proposed at the time, but it is hard to know how to account for that. True theories are better than false ones, but how can one false theory be better than another false theory. Is it less false? Is it more true? Is it closer to the truth? Do those ideas make any sense?

Chapter 10

Playing the Hobbes Game at Philosophy Camp

Robert K. Garcia

The Hobbes Game is designed to simulate what Thomas Hobbes (1588–1679) called *the state of nature*. This is a hypothetical state before humans formed civil societies, a violent state of competition driven by self-preservation, a state of "war of every man against every man," where one's existence is "solitary, poor, nasty, brutish, and short."

The original Hobbes Game was designed and published by John Immerwahr in 1976.[1] Others have gone on to revise and discuss the game, including Lee Archie (1995), Martin E. Gerwin (1996), Cristian Bellon (2001), and Ryan Pollock (2014).[2] Pollock's version is significantly different from Immerwahr's and I have used it successfully with undergraduates in an ethics course as well as with high school students in a philosophy camp. Below I will sketch Pollock's version of the game, explain its pedagogical value, describe its impact on campers, and offer some practical suggestions for gameplay. For game instructions and further discussion, please see Pollock's excellent article.

A SKETCH OF THE HOBBES GAME

Arguably, in an actual state of nature, resources (power, material goods, etc.) would be initially distributed in a random and unequal way. A virtue and distinctive feature of Pollock's version is its use of role-playing to simulate these initial conditions: each player is randomly assigned a character to play, and each character has unique strengths and weaknesses.

Pollock's game also simulates a state of nature by instructing each player to pursue their own self-interest, which the game quantifies with "glory points." Points are acquired through amassing resources—not only bread, water, shelter, lumber, and weapons but also the freedom and labor of other players. Whoever survives the game with the most glory points is the winner.

Because of the uneven initial playing field, the pursuit of individual survival and self-advancement requires significant engagement among players. Some of this can be friendly or neutral: trading, sharing, cooperating, promise keeping, forming alliances, and so on. But some of it can be downright hostile: attacking, taking someone's freedom, breaking a promise, betraying an alliance, and so on. Thus, gameplay is highly immersive, inevitably intense, and sometimes even chaotic.

THE PEDAGOGICAL VALUE OF THE GAME

Playing the Hobbes Game is an effective tool for teaching political philosophy, especially at a philosophy camp. I will describe several of the game's pedagogical virtues, from the more general to the more specific. First, it is highly immersive and the competitive nature of the game insures a high rate of engagement. It works well at the beginning of a camp or semester, not only as an icebreaker but also as a means to provide students with a large stock of shared experiences that can be mined and discussed throughout the camp (Archie 1995, p. 265). After playing the game, students are especially primed for more abstract thinking about political theory and the prisoner's dilemma.

Second, thinking realistically about political philosophy requires paying attention to the various conditions in which humans find themselves, such as being powerless or disadvantaged, being empowered or advantaged, being subject to inhumane treatment or betrayal, as well as what it is like to trust someone or betray someone's trust. Because it involves role-play, the Hobbes Game provides students with an effective opportunity to imagine and develop an empathetic understanding of some of those conditions. In this regard, the game facilitates self-knowledge—some students, for example, were surprised to discover how easily they betrayed others or, alternatively, how deferential they became in conflicts.

Third, the game engages a variety of learning styles. According to David Kolb, students learn by drawing upon the following four elements of experience.[3] The game engages each of them. Students who learn through *abstract conceptualization* have the opportunity to reflect on whether and how gameplay dynamics illustrate or can be explained by theoretical models. For example, the game naturally raises questions concerning whether psychological egoism is true and whether humans are social by nature (Aristotle) or only by practical necessity (Hobbes).

Students who learn through *concrete experience* benefit from the highly interactive gameplay. For example, players are drawn into making deals, forming alliances, taking risks—sometimes in secret and sometimes deceitfully.

Students who learn through *reflective observation* have the opportunity to watch and ponder the dynamic and complex human interactions that gameplay unfolds. For example, students can observe (and be subject to) the dynamics of self-interest, negotiation, loyalty, betrayal, and payback.

Finally, students who learn through *active experimentation* have the opportunity to devise, implement, and test various gameplay strategies. For example, a key tactical issue is whether or not to form an alliance to attack a more powerful player. Sometimes this works, but sometimes it backfires dramatically.

Fourth, the game provides both occasion and fodder for discussing a number of interrelated philosophical questions. Some of these concern the formation of *civil society*:

- What is human flourishing, and to what extent does it depend on things like chance, fortune, intelligence, hard work, initiative, friendships, and so on?
- What is fairness, and is it possible for humans to move from a state of nature to a fair civil society?
- Under what conditions and through what processes does civil society come about?
- What roles do self-interest, cooperation, and rationality play in the formation of civil society?

Other questions concern *human nature*:

- What are humans naturally like—Is there such a thing as human nature?
- What role does human nature play in the formation of civil society?

- What theories about human nature explain what happens when real individuals interact and especially when they attempt to cooperate or form a civil society?
- Is a human being "by nature a political animal," as Aristotle thought, or was Hobbes right that we only give up our freedom and form societies when it is mutually advantageous?
- Do people cooperate only when it is in their self-interest to do so?

Finally, some of the questions are about the *philosophical relevance of gameplay*:

- To what extent and in what ways can gameplay imitate the real dynamics of self-interest and cooperation?
- To what extent can gameplay provide a way to test philosophical ideas?
- Can simulations like the Hobbes Game tell us anything about human nature or the nature of political society?

THE IMPACT OF THE GAME

In my experience, playing the game impacts the students in a number of ways. I will mention two. First, the game gives life to the sorts of philosophical questions noted above. Indeed, it tends to lodge a number of them in the collective mind of the students, where they provoked discussion over the remainder of the camp or semester.

Second, the immediate emotional impact on the students can be mixed. Gameplay is not always pleasant for everyone—and this is by design. As Immerwahr said of his version, "A proper Hobbes game ought to bring out the worst in players rather than the best" (1976, p. 435). The students themselves see this dynamic. For example, one player hollered out, "You all don't even know me and you've already attacked me!" Not surprisingly, players who end up being betrayed or "enslaved" in gameplay sometimes report that although they did not enjoy the game, they found it highly worthwhile and would like to play it again.

SUGGESTIONS FOR PLAYING THE GAME

I will close with a few suggestions for running the game with your students:

- First, to understand the setup and rules for the game, please see Pollock's article.
- Second, I suggest creating and distributing a document that introduces the game prior to game day. In my experience, gameplay goes more smoothly if students have a chance to read over the rules in advance. I have created a document for this purpose, along with other ready-to-print game materials, and I would be happy to share them upon request.[4]
- Third, in Pollock's game, there are ten character roles to be played. If there are a few more than ten students, I would suggest asking students to pair up to play a single character. With groups of twenty to twenty-five students, I would suggest splitting the group in half and running two separate games at once.
- Finally, I suggest drawing attention to the fact that the rules do not prohibit promise-breaking, betrayal, or outright lying—all of these can happen without violating any of the official game rules. Of course, as students immediately see, these actions are risky and can backfire. Furthermore, although such actions are legal, students sometimes feel uncomfortable with the idea of attacking or betraying another player. As one student said, "It feels icky!" In light of this, at critical moments of gameplay (such as when players are negotiating a deal), I suggest reminding the players that there are no rules against making false promises. Not only does this increase the drama, it also helps students understand what a state of nature would be like and leads to gameplay that better simulates an unregulated pursuit of self-interest.

NOTES

1. Immerwahr, "The Hobbes Game," *Teaching Philosophy*, 1976 (1:4).

2. Lee C. Archie, An Analysis of "The Hobbes Game," *Teaching Philosophy*, 1995(18:3); Martin E. Gerwin, "The Hobbes Game, Human Diversity, and Learning Styles," *Teaching Philosophy*, 1996 (19:3); Christina Bellon, "At Play in the State of Nature: Assessing Social: Contract Theory Through Role Play," *Teaching*

Philosophy, 2001(24:4); Ryan Pollock, "Evaluating the State of Nature through Gameplay," *Teaching Philosophy*, 2014 (37:1).

3. These learning styles are taken from David Kolb's work as cited in Gerwin (1996). Here I am largely drawing upon and somewhat simplifying Gerwin's discussion of Immerwahr's game and learning styles. His discussion applies equally well to Pollock's version.

4. Feel free to e-mail me at Robert_K_Garcia@baylor.edu.

Chapter 11

Rational Choice Theory and the Prisoner's Dilemma

Cora Drozd

Buying out all the toilet paper in the midst of a pandemic. Worse, buying out hand sanitizers and selling them on Amazon for profit. These are instances that reveal, when under specific constraints, humans may act out of self-interest instead of the common interest. What are the motivations for these decisions? By maximizing our own gain, are we behaving rationally? Is this what we expect of human behavior? Can we trust that others will behave altruistically? Why might we show consideration for our fellow person? Must we be incentivized.

To direct young people toward this way of thinking, a thought experiment in the prisoner's dilemma is helpful. I have done variations of this exercise with different groups of students, and each time, I find that the students really engage with this topic.

The basic logic is this:

- A and B are charged with a robbery and are brought in separately for questioning.
- If A and B each betray the other, each of them serves two years in prison.
- If A betrays B but B remains silent, A will serve *no* time and B will serve three years in prison (and vice versa).
- If A and B both remain silent, both of them will serve only one year in prison.

This exercise requires not only that one think about what is best for her, but about what the other might do. To maximize personal utility, one must weigh her level of trust in the other. She might stay silent in hopes that he does too, because a one-year sentence is the lowest common denominator. However, he might not be thinking of the lowest common denominator, but rather of his utility-maximizing option. He will serve no time if he betrays her and she remains silent. But he risks her betraying him as well and getting more time than if they hadn't spoken at all. (It is not necessary to explain these scenarios with the rules—the idea is to elicit them after the exercise is completed through dialogue about the participants' own decision-making processes.)

To begin the lesson, simply explain the rules: if A and B betray each other and so on. It might be nice to have the rules written on the board or in a handout so the students can reference them. Then there are two possible approaches:

1. The group can be divided in half and tasked with making a decision as a collective. (In this case, give them time to discuss among themselves before bringing both groups together to explain their decision.)
2. It can be done as a series of mini exercises with two people standing back-to-back. By giving a thumbs-up, they are deciding to cooperate, and by giving a thumbs-down, they are making the decision to betray. They can turn around to see what the other has decided and a group discussion can be had once all the students have gone.

Alternatively, the rules could be oriented around incentives rather than punishment:

- If A and B each betray the other, each gets only one piece of candy.
- If A betrays B but B remains silent, A will get three pieces of candy while B will get none.
- If A and B both remain silent, both of them will get two pieces of candy.

While candy provides higher stakes, I have found that students actually prefer the hypothetical prison sentence—but if you wanted to try both variations and discuss responses to incentives versus punishment, that is a possibility.

THE PRISONER'S DILEMMA IN POPULAR CULTURE

Are we only out for ourselves? In the 2012 film, *The Dark Night Rises*, the Joker puts this to the test. In his experiment, he rigs two ferries leaving the city with explosives and gives each ferry the ultimatum: *You have a switch to detonate the other ship to save yourselves. If neither does so by midnight, I will detonate both ships.* On one ship there are civilians and on the other there are prisoners. This quandary opens serious considerations for the participants: Can the civilians trust the prisoners? Are the prisoner lives more dispensable? Can the prisoners trust the civilians?

There is a happy ending to this story. A prisoner throws his ship's detonator into the water, refusing to harm the civilians. When it seems as though the civilian ship might make the survivalist decision to detonate the other, the disgruntled civilian ultimately decides against it and they all live. The clip ends with the Batman telling the Joker, "This city just proved that it is full of people ready to believe in good."

REFLECTIONS

With permission from the teacher, I showed this clip in a high school classroom. I thought that using film as a stimulus for discussion might present philosophy in less abstract terms. The takeaways from this exercise are what I wish to share here; for better or for worse, they shaped my understanding of my role as facilitator. The teacher whose classroom I was visiting had attended several Philosophy for Children (P4C) teaching workshops but was hesitant to apply the pedagogy in her classroom. She said her students notoriously used physical aggression instead of words to solve disputes. I had been facilitating P4C discussions in a local school for some time, so I felt confident enough to do a demo lesson for this teacher.

Because this was my first time working with these students, I surveyed the room to see if anyone had any prior experience with philosophy. None had, so I asked them to share their understandings of the meaning of philosophy. I explained that philosophy entails asking questions that are open-ended—the question is philosophical because of the level at which it is asked. I said that we would watch the clip and open the floor for philosophical questions afterward.

This was a classroom comprising primarily racial minorities, and the Black Lives Matter movement was framing the public discourse at the time. Inevitably, the conversation went in the direction of police brutality, racial targeting, and mistrust of authority. There was a moment when the students started yelling back and forth and I was no longer in control. One student turned toward me to ask what the point was if we were just going to argue.

I began to explain what I previously thought was implicit—the aim was not to argue but to listen and to respond to another's perspective. I described the value that this form of discussion adds to democracy, and we wrapped up our discussion rather civilly. Afterward, one student approached me to say that they are not used to talking outside of their own friend groups.

In a similar instance in which I covered a controversial topic with a group of eighth graders, the outcome was different. We began with a discussion on implicit and explicit bias, which fed into a discussion on affirmative action. Where the conversation could have been deeply personal, the students were able to sustain an entirely philosophical discussion. The distinction I draw between this discussion and the one in the high school classroom is that these students had been doing philosophy for the better part of a year. Through routine lessons, they had developed the appropriate dispositions for doing philosophy.

When I started doing P4C, I was perhaps too encouraged by its novelty to recognize the foundations that need to be put in place for it to work. The experience I had in the high school classroom was critical for my realizing the importance of my own reflexivity. I learned not to assume that students demonstrate philosophical sensitivity automatically. Additionally, I learned that my position as facilitator is not a neutral one—my role in the discussion matters. The high schoolers might well have been hostile to the idea of an unfamiliar person in their classroom discussing something personal to them. Ideally, P4C breaks down these barriers, but some level of trust is required from the start.

Lesson learned: Do not discuss a provocative topic until a solid framework is in place. Gauge the level of experience your participants have with philosophy and your relationship to them, and choose an exercise based on these factors. Start with the Ship of Theseus or Plato's Cave Allegory and ease into lessons with more sensitive connotations.

CONCLUSION

If you are planning a P4C camp, you, like me, probably believe in the virtue of P4C. We acknowledge that it is provocative but endorse that it has generally constructive outcomes. This idea echoes Socrates's belief in the *elenchus*: what is initially destructive is, after all, productive. Thomas Jefferson has similar sentiments about the sum benefits of protest: "It will often be exercised when wrong, but better so than not to be exercised at all."[1] A contentious debate isn't exactly the aim of a P4C discussion, but through continuous P4C modeling, the goal is to enable productive dialogue about contentious issues. A camp is a ripe environment to build these skill sets.

A final recommendation I have is to go beyond the canon of P4C exercises by taking underlying concepts like rational choice theory or game theory and applying them in different contexts. For example, rational choice theory is great for thinking about privacy considerations online. That is, by accepting non-necessary advertising cookies (in effect, enabling targeted advertising) or by logging into apps using our Facebook information (effectively allowing big data to do its thing by creating a digital footprint), to what extent are we in control of our data? Are we merely pawns in all of this? Are advertisers and tech companies acting in our best interests? Do we have all the information needed to make the best decision for ourselves? The real-world implications vary depending on the stimulus you choose to use, but the logic is often the same. Don't be afraid to get creative. The more ways we can use philosophy to foster self-reflection, the better. (And we just might come out of a pandemic stronger.)

NOTE

1. Letter to Abigail Adams, February 22, 1787; reproduced in Thomas Jefferson, *Writings* (The Library of America, 1984), pp. 889–890.

Chapter 12

Philosophy, Magic, and Curiosity

Reflections on P4C Texas's 2019 Summer Camp

Michael Portal

The theme for Philosophy for Children (P4C) Texas's 2019 Summer Camp was J. K. Rowling's *Harry Potter*. This theme may not be intuitive because philosophy is often portrayed as the pure and disinterested articulation of reason, logic, and truth—as a deliberately abstract and, as a result, notoriously inaccessible area of study. The camp organizers sought to challenge this framing of philosophy by using moments from the best-selling young adult series *Harry Potter* to explore philosophy. The challenge: Can one really learn about philosophy by reading fantasy?

The success of P4C Texas's summer camp confirmed philosophy's radical potential to enable one of any age to make sense of the world, seek truth, and think critically, even when reading fantasy. More than this, the camp demonstrated how philosophy is without determinate form or content. Rather than reducing philosophy to the great works of past thinkers, P4C Texas utilized philosophy primarily as a method to cultivate and encourage the expression of one's innate curiosity. In this reflection on the modules I led for the 2019 Summer Camp, I explore P4C's profound commitment to this understanding of philosophy.

I

In general, philosophers take themselves very seriously, often endlessly debating the scope and limits of their discipline in an effort to justify their work. Unfortunately, these debates often obscure (or leave obscure) the realities that condition one's very access to the discipline. The systematic exclusion of certain issues, methods, and peoples from the discipline is often unexamined. Indeed, the discipline often claims that it is *has* to be exclusionary in order to properly define and to distinguish itself from other areas of study.

Western philosophers have worked to distance themselves from the world of fantasy and illusion, which they consider antithetical to rigorous philosophical thought. Consider Plato's Socrates who, in challenging the empty and bewitching words of the sophists, became a champion of reason and the dialectic. Today's philosopher might, likewise, contend that magic depends upon trickery and deception, or unspoken and inexplicable premises that are not open to critical analysis or reflection. A "scientific" study of magic would seem nonsensical or divorced from truth and reality, leaving it outside of philosophy's domain.

Thus, P4C Texas's *Harry Potter* summer camp is a provocation that highlights the arbitrary distinction between what is and is not philosophical, as well as who can and cannot become a philosopher. Such distinctions and oppositions are passed along by philosophy's practitioners as immutable truths: philosophy is today, seemingly without question, its own proper and professional discipline.

For many Western philosophers, it is simply "given" that only certain issues are legitimately philosophical and that only certain people (those who have read the right books, have the right educational pedigree, etc.) may be permitted to discuss them. P4C Texas's camp showcased that, in reality, philosophy is largely blind to these presuppositions.

P4C is an uncompromising challenge to this elitism, which has been used to prop up the discipline of philosophy for centuries. During P4C Texas's camp, middle school- and high school–aged campers were treated as intellectual peers by professors and graduate students who were genuinely eager to hear and engage with each camper's insights. Philosophical authority was decentered and philosophical inquiry democratized: philosophy was for everyone equally, no matter their training, race, gender, or age. In a discipline historically dominated by older white men, P4C Texas's camp provided an incredible opportunity to do philosophy differently.

What mattered most during this weeklong camp was not the traditional philosophical capital or pedigree but one's curiosity. In developing the camp's program, module leaders reflected on eternal philosophical questions and how similar questions circulate within Rowling's text. Each module was grounded in exciting and puzzling passages from the novels: passages that encouraged one to imagine, explore, and get lost in a fantastical world or situation. The modules would then deepen the discussion of Rowling's text by reflecting on how they exposed unarticulated assumptions or other initially obscure facts about the real world.

Classical philosophical issues were revealed as the undercurrent present within Rowling's text. To demonstrate this, each module centered on an exegetical discussion of a passage from *Harry Potter* that was then developed by reading a more traditional or canonical philosophical work. These supplementary texts provided analytic tools or alternative methods of interpretation to the inquisitive and engaged reader. The two texts amplified each other, encouraging the campers to be curious and imaginative, to explore new and unknown connections—in short, to ask questions.

Philosophy, in this setting, plays upon one's imagination and inquisitiveness. Everything is open to question, even the most familiar texts and obvious truths. By taking *Harry Potter*, a text that was already meaningful to the campers, as our starting point for philosophical inquiry, we were set to reimagine philosophy. Philosophy was not a set of canonical truths or systems that served to grant the text its meaning. Instead, philosophy was a tool used to bring to the fore the already present meaning of the text. Philosophy was a new way to explore meaning: to look at the world in new ways, making it unfamiliar in order to provoke exploration and reflection.

However, one might ask, "Does this approach dilute the rigorous study of philosophy?" Our answer: "No." The camp staff took the theme as a unique opportunity: that we began with something so familiar and well-read allowed us to dive even deeper into the philosophical undertones of Rowling's text and philosophy more generally. Her books already had the philosophy in them, so our job was easy—we just had to help the campers uncover the philosophical richness of the text and draw out the connections between Rowling's text and its more traditional and philosophical referents. In this way, Rowling's novels made good philosophy possible.

One of the camp's main goals was to get the campers to realize that philosophy isn't just in Plato: it is in everything they already consume and care about. The selected supplemental readings, then, were indispensable. The previously immutable borders between philosophy and everything else (deceptive magic, popular literature, etc.) were necessarily blurred as campers found each text (Rowling's "parent text" and the supplemental reading) exciting because of how the texts related to and enriched one another. Philosophy was divorced from its canon and presented as a method of inquiry, of revisiting familiar and beloved passages to rethink and reflect on one's knowledge and understanding.

Still, one might ask, "How significant can philosophy really be to middle school and high school students crammed into a university classroom during their summer break?" My modules attempted to answer this question. I organized the modules and selected readings to play on the campers' curiosity and test their willingness to find more meaning in the pages of books that most of them had read many times over. To really test the limits of such philosophical discussion, I paired Rowling's text (and some clips from the movie adaptation) with the works of abstruse twentieth-century French philosophers. This was a gamble.

II

My modules began by establishing rules to govern our discussion. I used this opportunity to performatively shift and challenge camper expectations. Rules were not imposed by an authority figure in the room but reflected collective decision-making and consensus. I quickly typed the campers' proposed rules for discussion into a document projected on a whiteboard.

Consider the camper-proposed rule: "Pay attention." The campers determined that just paying attention or merely hearing another's comments were not enough. Instead, we should try to "listen" to each other and, since understanding is never promised, make sure we were at least "*open* to understanding" each other. The rule was refined accordingly. (Emphasis mine)

Rules Governing Discussion Created by Middle School Campers

1. No rude comments.
2. Try not to talk over others (interrupt).

3. Do not dominate the conversation (one person talking, "Shut up I am not done").
4. Pay attention (make sure you are listening = open to understanding).
5. Keep an open mind and don't impose your view on another.
6. No phones unless absolutely necessary.
7. Be respectful = do not raise your voice.

The high school campers developed similar rules of discourse and self-governance. Here, the opening deliberation centered on the importance of having rules at all: Is there a meaningful difference between rules that are imposed by others and those of our own creation? Do they both restrict our freedom in the same way?

Rules Governing Discussion Created by High School Campers

1. No killing, violence, and so on (be respectful).
2. No phones.
3. Refer to people by name.
4. Rules that are imposed = negate freedom.
5. You have elected these rules = freedom.

As with the middle schoolers, I quickly wrote down and helped refine each camper's contribution. While I did ask clarifying questions and tried to synthesize different threads of thought, I existed primarily as a scribe and as a facilitator for an organic discussion that both the middle school and high school campers wanted to have—and one that they had already begun.

In this way, a simple exercise to determine rules eliminated the need for (or perceived presence of) an authoritarian pedagogue. Each student felt encouraged to contribute because they determined the direction of the discussion; their contributions, like everyone else's, made it onto the screen to shape the written record. More than this, because each contribution was subject to refinement, the campers felt responsible for improving the document that they developed together. Since the document was open to endless revision, the students were given the chance to make mistakes without consequence or fear of censure: to explore *and* get lost.

This document served as a record of the students' exegetical work as we then read from *Harry Potter*. In one module we took turns reading out loud about Harry Potter's oppressive family and how his flight to a magical boarding school functions as a necessary form of escapism. With reference to the text (which was presented with numbered lines for easy reference), the campers reconstructed the plot summary and answered tough questions about its meaning. As they were offered, the campers' contributions were put onto the screen, allowing the students to take charge of their own interpretation and reflect on that of their peers.

The campers' interpretations were read alongside Rowling's text, which offered the students a novel opportunity to see how their interpretation diverged from exact wording of the "parent text." For example, students who felt as if they knew the text well had difficulty identifying exactly which lines justified their understanding, especially as a multiplicity of interpretations began to bubble up. Certain questions became unavoidable: Was there a true and unassailable meaning to Rowling's words? What was beyond interpretation? As the students worked to decipher the text, students began to think creatively and consider other possible ways of reading—and justifying their reading—of the work. As a result, even the familiar pages of *Harry Potter* became unfamiliar and mysterious.

Here, P4C's reimagining of the philosophical task becomes most clear: philosophy is the decision to return to and rethink that which is most familiar to us and to that which, upon further reflection, is never as familiar as we might have suspected. What is truly philosophical, I found when observing the campers, was the willingness to be curious and to take nothing as self-evident or given. Rather than a set of canonical and eternal truths, philosophy was a *way* of exploring the world, of looking at it from new angles and through new lenses. As students worked to justify their reading of Rowling's text, the campers became increasingly involved in philosophical thought as new questions and understandings inevitably immerged from behind old and well-known pages.

Following this treatment of the Rowling text (our "parent text"), we transitioned to the supplementary text: a selection from Michel Foucault's "Of Other Spaces: Utopias and Heterotopias," which outlines the important role "heterotopias" (or "counter-sites") play in preserving imagination.[1] The campers used the skills they just developed while reading Rowling to work through Foucault's dense style. Referencing particular lines from Foucault's text as necessary, students reconstructed his argument and developed an interpretation of it. Relating Foucault back to Rowling, campers realized

Harry Potter's escape to his boarding school, Hogwarts, as an escape to his own heterotopia.

The camper's interpretations of the text were tested, refined, and recontextualized to present the supplementary text's meaning in a more accessible idiom: While Harry Potter might have Hogwarts, what spaces or countersites are available to *us*? By reading Rowling and Foucault sequentially, the campers realized the importance of the text (in general) and the opportunities these particular texts afforded attentive and curious readers. The difficult task of developing and articulating one's interpretation—while realizing all the other possible interpretations—was not easy. It didn't matter what the students read, or if it was even a "proper" philosophical text, the actual act of "philosophy" was tied to the endless and rigorous refinement and reexamination of one's interpretation.

Since the campers realized that there was (and is) no predetermined end to the philosophical and interpretative task that lay before them, they were liberated to make mistakes and contribute without fear of judgment. There was always more to question and explore, no matter how much they refined and developed their understanding. Thus, campers were forced to realize the normative importance of interpretation, that we *must* always continue to ask questions and interpret if we want to seek truth. In this way, the use of Foucault's philosophy and Rowling's novel were effective as both texts required the campers to develop a willingness to meticulously read and reread, always digging for deeper meaning.

I intentionally selected texts and passages that lent themselves to this type of layering. The short excerpt from Foucault, for example, is complex but uses familiar imagery that captivates the imagination. By emphasizing this imagery, even the most difficult and confusing moments of the text become accessible. After all, campers were already well acquainted with mirrors and dreams of pirate ships—the images Foucault uses to describe "heterotopias." Because the campers were familiar with Foucault's imagery, they had a way into the text and the explanation of the world that it was offering—the campers now felt empowered to help chart the world of the text.

Using familiar images or metaphors (in Foucault) and texts that campers had already read (like Rowling's) encouraged participation and made the philosophical task and text approachable. My original goal, however, was to find the limits of the campers' philosophical interests and to see if they were capable of seeing philosophy everywhere. So, in my second module, I dealt more explicitly with the issue of familiarity. I was concerned that the familiar superseded the unfamiliar, and perhaps the campers were using philosophy to talk about *Harry Potter* and not using *Harry Potter* to talk about or *do* philosophy. Perhaps, my gamble to discuss French philosophy did not actually pay off or challenge the campers to think creatively and make new connections. To my relief, this was not the case as was demonstrated by the campers' engagement with my second module.

In the second module, we read aloud a scene in which Harry Potter acquires a magical map that reveals the location of all who wander about Hogwarts. This map discloses special or privileged information that could be used to spy on others, escape detection, or aid in a variety of (licit or illicit) activities. The familiar boarding school becomes unfamiliar as Harry Potter uses the map to navigate it differently. This magical map immediately provokes questions from the middle schoolers about knowledge itself: What does it mean to know something or to know something well? Can the mere possession of knowledge be dangerous or criminal?

Again, thoughtful selection of the supplemental reading was critical. In this module, I paired *Harry Potter* with selections from Michel de Certeau's *The Practice of Everyday Life*.[2] This discussion encouraged campers to explore what it would mean to have special, exclusive, or privileged information and how having such information might change how they lived in the world. After all, the world could become familiar or unfamiliar because of what one knows or doesn't know about it.

We focused on one of Certeau's most famous examples in which he distinguishes between the perspective of someone standing atop the World Trade Center (knowledge from the grand view) and the perspective of someone walking the bustling streets down below. Each perspective shapes a particular interpretation or understanding of the city's reality. While, certainly, the perspective from above provides unique information about the world (one can see the "strategy" and planning of the city), this does not diminish the significance of the lived reality in the streets (the "tactics" someone needs to navigate crowded sidewalks). For Certeau, those walking the city streets are the ones who write the city's "text," all while being unable to read what they write.

In reconstructing Certeau's argument, the middle schoolers were confronted by serious and deep philosophical questions about how to read and write a text. How is the city a type of text? How are those walking in the city "writing" that text? For the creative reader, imagining oneself as a bird in the sky and looking down on the city is both easy and informative. The imagery that Certeau uses is helpful and suggests different layers of meaning. Still, these images are not necessarily enough to make sense of the unfamiliar ways that Certeau talks about the city as a text, the walker as a writer, and so on. Certeau's example might feel impenetrable, even if the imagery is not.

Put another way, had we presented Certeau's text in a purely academic idiom or context the campers might have felt unable to participate in the discussion of the text or develop their own interpretation of it. Instead, by reading the text alongside excerpts from *Harry Potter*, the campers immediately saw what it would be like to populate a text (or map) by simply living life. Harry Potter's map reveals everyone's location—the footsteps of a meandering student or pacing professor supply the map with its content in real time. A camper proposed a real-life correlate: modern surveillance, and how one's cell phone leaves a digital trace that could also be used to map or plot one's whole life. One's life (their story) becomes a text to be read like all the others.

Following this camper's intervention (which, in my eyes, demonstrated a deep understanding of the underlying and real philosophical issues at work in Rowling's world), the discussion shifted to a brief assessment of surveillance and the collection and use of privileged information. Slowly, as Certeau's text became more familiar, students more willingly shared their thoughts on the phenomenological aspects of Certeau's example (about what it was really like to be at the top of a building, to look down on a crowd, to feel tracked, etc.). I continued, as the scribe, to write down this discussion, clarifying and refining each interpretation in the document I had projected on the wall. The document was slowly taking a form of its own.

Not long afterward, a certain awareness came over some of the campers: they realized that they, too, were writing a text. In struggling through the difficult and endless interpretative task, the campers had unwittingly drafted their own metatext in the projected document. Thus, the second module played on the campers' desire to cling to what is familiar: the common way of using a map, walking down the street, and so on. Critically returning to and playing on this tendency, the module suggested that the campers explore unfamiliar territory, draft their own map, and reflect on what they had made:

a map that had, at once, become familiar (our own) just as it was able to make the strange texts familiar to us.

Thus, the texts I selected used familiar images in unfamiliar ways to introduce philosophy as a particular type of activity or method, a way of making the world both strange and familiar: as something worth reflecting upon and questioning. The campers' natural curiosity, unsurprisingly, took over and led to an introspective moment where the campers caught sight of what they were doing (as they made their own map and text) and eventually saw themselves as "proper" philosophers.

III

I doubt that philosophy is something one "does" by reading the right books or using the right idioms. Perhaps philosophy is something that simply "happens" in those moments of life when one has the time, will, and curiosity to be introspective. Here, I have discussed how P4C recasts philosophy as way of thinking and asking questions, of allowing oneself to make something familiar strange in order to understand it more profoundly. Philosophy, therefore, is not predetermined or restricted to certain classically philosophical issues, only to be accessible to those with college degrees. P4C Texas's 2019 Summer Camp demonstrated that the endless philosophical and interpretative task is one that is exciting and possible for everyone.

My modules invited campers to ask questions and be curious without fear of judgment. By disappearing into the background as a scribe, the campers' discussions were organic and unguided. As the campers conversed and made sense of the texts we read, I contemporaneously typed their words into a document projected on the wall. The campers ultimately realized that their recorded interpretations themselves became a text and that they were responsible for having collaboratively written some philosophy, of having made sense of difficult and strange texts.

In these moments of clarity, the arbitrary and stodgy distinctions between what is and is not philosophical, between who can and cannot be a philosopher, had to be rethought. After all, it was abundantly clear that middle school- and high school-aged campers were asking meaningful questions and doing good philosophy—all while discussing magic.

NOTES

1. Michel Foucault, "Of Other Spaces: Utopias and Heterotopias" in *Rethinking Architecture: A Reader in Cultural Theory*, ed. Neil Leach (New York: Routledge/ Taylor & Francis, 2005), 330–336. We did not read the whole essay, only select passages. The most sustained and significant passages we discussed are found on 332 (beginning "First of all, the utopias.") and 336 (beginning "Brothels and colonies, here are two extreme types of heterotopia.").

2. Michel de Certeau, *The Practice of Everyday Life* (Berkeley and Los Angeles, California: University of California Press, 1988), 91–110. We read and discussed selections from chapter seven, "Walking in the City." The most sustained and significant passages we discussed are found on 91 (beginning "Seeing Manhattan from the 110th floor of the World Trade Center."), 92 (beginning "To be lifted to the summit of the World Trade Center."), and 93 ("The ordinary practitioners of the city. Live 'down below,' below the thresholds at which visibility begins.").

Chapter 13

The If/Then Exercise and the Case for Incorporating P4C into Pre-K Camps and Programs

Charles Royal Carlson

Even though a preschool camp in philosophy might be a tall task, there is good reason to include P4C activities in any camp or routine gathering of preschoolers. One of the driving ideas behind P4C is that philosophical inquiry should not be withheld from the young. If we disregard Aristotle's supposed suggestion that you have to be forty to have the wisdom and experience needed to engage in the process, then the next question becomes, when is the right age to begin?

From the facilitator's side there are certainly good reasons to wait until children are a little more patient and have the vocabulary needed to participate in vigorous discussion. However, from the child's perspective, the ability to ask questions, give reasons, and understand the reasons of others is a skill that they demand as soon as they are able to express interest in the world around them.

Evidence in favor of doing P4C is usually the result of studies done with older age groups, but the reasoning and social emotional skills that are shown to benefit from P4C are just as important for the youngest of children. The inability to explain feelings and tell others what they see as problematic is the source of many frustrations, and is especially so for pre-K children who do not yet have the tools to even begin the process. One study done with pre-K children bears this out, noting that after participating in a P4C program,

The main results indicated that philosophical group discussions, guided according to P4C, significantly increased the children's responses containing logical comparison, analogy, contrast, justification, causal connections and . . . P4C also increased the children's talkativeness, but decreased the amount of incoherent responses, responses like "I don't know," and direct descriptions of the picture presented in the tests.[1]

For the past three years *P4C Texas* has been working with four and five year olds at Texas A&M University's Becky Gates Children Center. The thirty-minute sessions on Wednesdays are conversational and guided by a set of rules modified for this age group: listen to others, be respectful when responding, wait for your turn to speak, think about what you are going to say before you say it, and have fun. Our goal is to help them learn how to ask questions, give explanations for their answers, and listen and incorporate different explanations from others. These are the exact same things that work with P4C in older age groups.

Many barriers exist when doing P4C with the youngest of children; they often have difficulty differentiating a question from a statement, have difficulty understanding causal relationships, have significant vocabulary limitations, and have varying attention spans. And yet, the natural inquisitiveness and philosophical ability is very much present at this age and they are enthusiastic and indefatigable in their pursuit of answers.

These challenges can be overcome by establishing shared vocabulary and repeating familiar processes from week to week. For example, we start every session going over the rules, and asking if they remember what we did the previous week. It often takes a while for the pattern to become familiar to them, but there is one exercise in particular that we repeat with regularity to help them establish the basics and a shared set of terms we can build from.

The exercise is the "If/Then game." The purpose of this game is to help them experiment with causal relations and to practice giving reasons and explanations for the connections that they are making in their mind and expressing them verbally to others. We use a modified version of the exercise developed by The Preschool Project by Thomas E. Jackson and the UHM Children's Center as part of the exceptional Hawaii P4C program.

We use three pieces of paper to tell a story. The first is a large piece of paper taped to a wall where we will visually draw the story as it unfolds. The other two are colored half sheets of paper, the first says, "How Come?," and the second says, "Because . . . ." We start the story for them with something relevant to a book we recently read or whatever theme the class has been working on.

For instance, if it is raining we might say start by saying, "It is raining and Steve is outside." Then we turn complete and total control over to them. "If it is raining and Steve is outside, then . . . ," and they fill in the rest. Or, "If Becky has lost her stuffed animal at the park, then . . . " After they tell us what happens next, we ask them "How Come?" and instruct them to start their explanation with "Because." One by one they add to the story and the stories they tell are always quite fantastically complex and usually quite humorous. On more than a few occasions they have ended up in outer space.

As they are working through the steps of what happens next the facilitator illustrates the story on the sheet of paper taped to the wall. This allows the children to practice following the conversation and keeping the whole of the story in their head. A vital component of any good community of inquiry dialogue is the perception that some kind of progress is being made by the group, especially if there is no predetermined end state of the discussion.

The exercise also allows them to become comfortable explaining why they are thinking what they are thinking. The act of telling the group why they think something should happen next makes it easier to do so in the future, and results in less shoulder shrugging and "I don't know" responses.

When we start discussing more directly philosophically oriented discussion topics, this exercise provides a lodestone for how the process goes, and allows them to practice giving explanations that don't have the emotional weight of other topics. Importantly, the exercise is very enjoyable for the children and something they often request if we haven't done in a while.

The challenges of doing P4C with preschool-aged children become insignificant when compared with the benefits of helping the young mind put words to their wonder. Once they have the basic tools to express the inherent inquisitiveness that they have about the largely unknown world around them they blossom into fairly excellent conversationalists who consistently experience the joy of metacognitive moments of insight. Even though we are only with them a total of two hours a month, the progress they make is clear and significant.

In summary, the value of incorporating P4C into any pre-K program or camp far outdistances the relatively small cost in time invested into the process. Through regular sessions that establish familiarity with asking questions, giving reasons, learning to play, and be flexible in their cognitive processes, and practice listening and understanding others, even pre-K children are able to get the benefits of P4C, perhaps even more than older children.

NOTE

1. "Improving Pre-Schoolers' Reasoning Skills Using the Philosophy for Children Programme" Egle Säre, Piret Luik, and Tiia Tulviste—*TRAMES*, 2016, 20(70/65), 3, 273–295.

Chapter 14

Teaching Freire

Philosophy for Children Lesson

Ana Olivares-McFadden

Category: education, teacher/student relationship.

Target age group: sixth grade and older.

Lesson objective: Students will explore their educational experiences by analyzing Freire's banking concept of education by considering how their schooling relates to Freire's model.

Key concept: Freire's Banking Concept of Education (*Pedagogy of the Oppressed by Paulo Freire*, Chapter 2). Paulo Freire. *Pedagogy of the Oppressed*. Bloomsbury Academic, 2018, p. 73.

- In the banking concept of education, the teacher-student relationship is an oppressive relationship involving the teacher as a narrative subject and the student as a passive object.
- The oppressive attitudes and practices of banking education:
  - The teacher teaches and the students are taught;
  - the teacher knows everything and the students know nothing;
  - the teacher thinks and the students are thought about;
  - the teacher talks and the student listen—meekly;
  - the teacher disciplines and the students are disciplined;
  - the teacher chooses and enforces his choice, and the students comply;
  - the teacher acts and the students have the illusion of acting through the action of the teacher;
  - the teacher chooses the program content, and the students (who were not consulted) adapt to it;

- the teachers confuses the authority of knowledge with his or her own professional authority, which she and he sets in opposition to the freedom of the students;
- the teacher is the Subject of the learning process, while the pupils are mere objects. (p. 73)

Seed question: Consider how Freire's banking concept of education relates to your schooling experience.

Discussion points:

- Describe your education.
- Describe your role as a student in a classroom.
- Describe your teacher's role in a classroom.
- What is the relationship between school life and home life?
- What roles do administrators, politicians, and so on play in education?
- How would you describe the content of your education?
- Who should determine what students learn?
- What is the purpose of education?
- What is the purpose of schooling?
- What characteristics/behaviors in students and teachers are encouraged/repressed?
- Any questions raised or issues discussed can be recorded so students can access them while they complete the activity.

Activity: Design your own school.

- Determine the purpose of your education and the pedagogical method to be implemented. Consider how the physical layout will influence your approach to education. Who are the teachers? Who are the students? Other considerations include location, food, recreation, schedule, community, and so on.
- Students can work in pairs (or in small groups up to four) to design their school.
- Students can create a poster (video, drawing, etc.) to present the school they designed.

Closure: Students will present their school design to the larger group and return to any questions raised during the discussion.

- What kind of issues did they come across?
- How does their school differ from traditional schooling? From the banking concept?
- If their school was meant to improve upon traditional schooling, how did they go about that?

Part III
CAMPER/PARENT OBSERVATIONS

Chapter 15

Camper and Parent Essays

AGGIE SCHOOL OF ATHENS, TEXAS A&M UNIVERSITY

Leaving the Cave—Further Reflections[1]
Evelyn Conway, Camper
High School Class of 2022

I was asked to write about what philosophy camp theme had the greatest impact on me. As I wrote in my original version of this essay, published in *Growing Up with Philosophy Camp* (Rowman & Littlefield, 2020), when I first attended philosophy camp in 2016, I had just finished sixth grade. I had some idea of what philosophy was since both of my parents teach philosophy at the university in the town where I live. I was excited to attend philosophy camp even though I knew I would be nervous to contribute my ideas to the discussion. I was not sure if I would be very good at this. I was not sure if my ideas would be taken seriously, or if I would have anything important to contribute. But those concerns were quickly put to rest.

The first thing we did on the first day of that first philosophy camp was watch what the staff refer to as "the creepy claymation" (the phrase used by the philosophy camp staff) video of Plato's Allegory of the Cave.[2] And then we had a discussion about it, first as a large group with the whole camp, and then in our smaller groups: middle school (where I was at the time) and high school. I didn't realize then how much of an impact on me that video and the themes we discussed would have, but I realize now looking back on that day, that I "see" the cave allegory everywhere.

The first time I applied themes from the cave allegory was that first afternoon of philosophy camp. We watched an episode of the PBS series *Brain Games* on sex/gender differences. During the discussion, my campmates expressed the view that there were no differences between the sexes. Whether that claim is true is for another time. But during our discussion in 2016, the facilitator asked us to look around the room and talk about how we were sitting. It took us a little while, but eventually we realized that we were sitting in clusters of boys and clusters of girls. "Why are you sitting in this arrangement?" the facilitator asked.

Her question led us to a discussion about friendship and the assumptions that we make about our friends of the same sex. I realized then, at that moment, that how we think about our relationships with other people is one of our intellectual chains. Why do we view people in particular ways? Are we trapped in this thinking? What would it take to break those chains? How do we break chains that we do not even know we have?

But as I wrote in my original essay, I apply themes from Plato's cave allegory to everything, literally, everything. I see the cave allegory in books I read and conversations that I have. I saw it in *Lord of the Flies*, in *The Joy Luck Club*, and in *A Separate Peace*. For example, in *A Separate Peace*, I thought their cave was the school. At one point in the story, Leper left to go into the military, similar to the person in the allegory who leaves the cave. Gene visits Leper after Leper is discharged from the military, and Leper tells Gene how horrible the military is, how horrible war is.

But everyone at the school can't wait to do this—this is what they are taught, and this is all they know—and so Gene does not believe Leper. He even calls Leper crazy—just like in the cave allegory. The chains on their thinking were their beliefs about the war, and these beliefs were reinforced by their experiences in school. I don't know if the comparison fits perfectly, but I can see pieces of it. The larger lesson about being chained, about not knowing or not wanting to know is present in all of these books. I also see it in discussions I have with people. It is clear that they sometimes don't want to know the truth. They would rather stay chained.

Watching the video of the cave allegory on the first day of the camp week is now a tradition, even this summer although we had to have our camp discussions over Zoom. We still took that time, watched the video together, and then had a discussion. Five times we have viewed that video and we still find something new to discuss. Every summer we see something we didn't see the previous summer. Of course, every summer, we have also changed. We are a year older, a year wiser. As different people we can't help either to see themes in the video from a different perspective or to see themes that we didn't see at all in previous summers.

I am about to begin my junior year of high school. And while I understand why philosophy might not be taught in my school, I decided that philosophy camp did not need to be the only place we had these discussions and created this community. This past year I started a philosophy club at school so that we could continue these dialogues outside of philosophy camp and maybe introduce others to the importance of having these discussions. My friends and I are learning how to leave the cave, and with each other's help, we just might succeed.

No Red Pens: Philosophy Camp Brings Learning Back to Life

Calla Duffield, Camper

Texas A&M University's philosophy camp isn't just about learning the names of philosophers or their history, although that is part of it. It is mostly about discovering how to think. For me, philosophy camp is the embodiment of a quote by Plato (my favorite philosopher): "Do not train a child to learn by force or harshness; but direct them to it by what amuses their minds, so that you may be better able to discover with accuracy the peculiar bent of the genius of each."

Never have I enjoyed any type of classroom-learning that consists solely of being talked at. To be honest, when I first heard about philosophy camp, I wasn't keen on spending a week of my summer in a situation much like school, with its classrooms and seven-hour days.

Much to my relief, that is not what philosophy camp is about. It is a forum through which many ideas and issues can be discussed, such as the true purpose of education, whether political parties are useful or harmful, and how to live together when we are all so different, topics we explored in last year's camp.

I first attended philosophy camp in 2018. I had no idea what we would be doing there, but I went because it was being run by Dr. Claire Katz, a friend of my mom's. Dr. Katz is Jewish, as is my family, and she is a philosophy professor who is well known for her work in Philosophy for Children.

The first day of camp, I arrived late to Rudder Tower, our designated meet-up spot, and a counselor took me and a few other late-comers to our classroom in the old YMCA building where we sat with about sixty middle and high school students. We did the usual thing when in groups like this: Said our name, age and an interesting fact about ourselves.

Then a professor of philosophy at Texas A&M came in and presented our first discussion topic (possibly the most well known in the world of philosophy): The Allegory of the Cave by Plato. The professor showed us a Claymation depiction of the allegory and asked for our thoughts. We talked about the Allegory of the Cave throughout the entire week of camp and never ran out of things to say. This first day really sparked my interest in Plato. We talked a lot about the purpose of education and how one learns, including a discussion about Plato's theory that when we learn, we really are just remembering what we already know.

Because I felt intimidated by the mass of forty or so campers in my middle school group, I said little for the first few days. Every day, a new professor or counselor would facilitate discussions, and sometimes we would undertake activities relating to a text, or split into smaller groups. By the middle of the week, however, a particular topic caught my interest: the movie, *The Matrix*, and whether campers would choose to take the red pill or blue pill. (For those who don't know, in the movie *The Matrix*, the main character has a choice: take the blue pill and continue to be unaware of the prison that surrounds him, or take the red pill, see life for what it is, and discover that he is in the matrix.)

Campers verbally rioted; students metaphorically threw food, toppled desks, and tore up papers because they were so invested in their opinions and working to convince others. When a hypothetical situation can get a group of kids that riled up, it has clearly struck a vein of philosophical conversation gold. There was another reason these discussions stood out to me: the professors and facilitators didn't try to guide or direct our discussions. They let us explore our ideas and didn't mold them or lead us to a conclusion but, rather, let us reach our own. For the first time in a while I spoke out about my thoughts without worrying about being right, because in philosophy, there are no right answers.

The 2019 camp group was a bit smaller—thirty-five or so campers in total. I loved the smaller size because it was easier to pose questions to the group as a whole and hear everyone's ideas. But when I found out that the theme of the 2019 camp was the *Harry Potter* book series, I was nervous, since I have never read any of the books. Although I did get a few "WHAT?? You've never read *Harry Potter*?," I was able to follow and participate in everything. The philosophical questions involving *Harry Potter* included the following: How does magical ability (or not having it) create social differences; what is the significance of Voldemort being a "half-blood" and how does gender impact Hermione's education and friendships at Hogwarts?

Discussions of the mythical world of *Harry Potter* often warped into comparisons with our own world. It turned out that the *Harry Potter* books are packed with philosophy, which we dissected in theatrical skits at the end of camp. But before we did so, the directors of the camp had professional wizardry professors from the Worthwich School of Wizarding teach wand-building to get us into the magical spirit—and then we got to make our own! After my enlightening experience at camp I happily accepted an invitation from the camp director, Dr. Katz, to join the philosophy camp board. In meetings, we usually analyze a text and then watch a movie and discuss it.

The most recent meeting was my second. It began with me texting my mom "ahhh get me out of here!" and ended with me recounting to my whole family the group's analysis of a Cain and Abel text from the Bible. We dissected the way the killing is described, whether Cain even knew what death was, and how interesting it is that there are a few words left out right before Abel is killed. This made me realize that it is important not to always take words literally, and that dissecting words in texts is crucial to understanding their meaning.

It may not seem interesting when English teachers spend whole class periods on the significance of the wind in an obligatory schoolbook, but this was different. Every camper had different opinions on the meaning of the text, and for some discussions we had to map out our thoughts on a white board because they were so vast and would otherwise become tangled up.

For me, there is nothing more wonderful than the feeling after a thoughtful discussion, when your brain is abuzz and almost overflowing and you need to get to a pen and paper as quickly as possible before all your epiphanies float away. Having that feeling every day of philosophy camp or after board meetings is worth more than words can describe. The most amazing thing about it is the intense learning created through conversation alone. In school, being forced to follow a rubric and having every drop of creativity squashed with red pen can be soul crushing. Thanks to philosophy camp providing room for individual expression and unbounded exploration, I can think for myself again.

The Things We Don't Talk About

Ellie Hague, Camper

There are some things you don't talk about. You never talk politics with your grandparents or discuss religion in school. It's not because either of these topics are inherently bad; rather, most people don't know how to have a real conversation, a conversation beyond "small talk." Too often, a conversation is more like people just stating their opinion; they are not trying to be genuinely open and listen to the other side.

Before going to philosophy camp, I was a very different person. I was one of those people who did not know how to listen; I only knew how to state my opinion. Yes, at philosophy camp, I learned about various existential questions and the responses. These themes are important to me. However, the most valuable, precious jewel I found at philosophy camp was the ability to listen to the other side. No matter what the debate was, philosophy camp created the right climate to nurture respect for others opinions.

Philosophy camp is a vastly different intellectual environment from the traditional public school. At philosophy camp there was no pressure of grades or of being judged in any way. Campers were allowed to speak freely and openly. In school there is only right and wrong, one plus one is two. School must be this way in order to measure improvement and retention of information. But in philosophy camp, you weren't just guessing for the right answer. Nothing was ever wrong—not in the school kind of way—so anything was always possible. One could begin to explore common topics and reach a new level knowledge. Conversations would spark during group discussions and slowly grow into a blaze, carrying over into meal times or walking to another building.

Discussion leaders would also accommodate discussions for various personality types. For example, I like to contribute to a discussion, but I take some time to formulate my thoughts. If I wanted to make a comment, I would simply raise my hand. I would be recognized by the facilitator and then state my thoughts. Typically, more extroverted people are more likely to express their opinion, and then take over a conversation. The moderation of the discussion by the experienced discussion leaders allowed everyone to be heard.

This experience helped me to recognize that just because someone does not contribute to a conversation, does not mean the person is not learning or growing from that experience. There is another camper who almost never raises his hand during the large group discussions. However, I noticed that when we are in smaller groups, he contributes. What I discovered in these small-group discussions is that this camper has interesting and enlightening reasons and thoughts. He just feels more comfortable simply listening in a large group. This accommodation—large groups and smaller groups—for different learning styles and modes of expression is one of the practices that sets the philosophy camp apart from any other camp.

Creating a nurturing environment that fosters the idea of growth and discovery enables campers to learn new and inspiring topics in safe, welcoming, and low-pressure environment. This experience allows campers to express themselves effectively. Teaching young people how to have a real discussion without getting angry and while respecting others' viewpoints is something that is lacking in schools and other learning environments. This is what makes philosophy camp so unique—it teaches kids understanding, not just facts.

Reflections of a Self-Proclaimed Nerd

Mia Paulk, Camper
High School Class of 2022

I was the weird kid. You know, that girl who sits in the front of the class, answering all the questions. Drawing dragons on the margins of my paper and, most importantly, the one asking all the questions. Why something was, who did what, what is the meaning of that? Sometimes, the teacher didn't even know how to answer. I was one of the students who actually cared about asking questions, for the simple reason of understanding why.

Not many high schoolers know what philosophy is. I know I didn't. We usually just picture Greek guys with thick beards waiting for someone to carve a marble sculpture of them. When I first heard about philosophy camp, it wasn't the "philosophy" part that interested me, it was the kids that would be there. It sounded incredible, the thought of being with other people who liked questioning hard truths and bending the way we understand the world.

I believe the most impactful aspect of philosophy camp was the ability to interact with people who were like you. The funny thing is, on the surface, we were all different. We all had opinions on politics, religion, morals, ethics, and the overall meaning of life. Yet we all shared this one binding characteristic; we wanted to know why. We wanted to ask questions, to understand, and rebel against common belief. In this way, we had the common goal of acquiring knowledge.

This is why it was so crucial to create an environment where it is ok for people to disagree. "What happens at philosophy camp stays at philosophy camp," was often jokingly said before a discussion, because it alleviates the social pressures we have when expressing our opinions. In this way, kids can learn how to express themselves adequately to a crowd, in addition to considering viewpoints they may not agree with.

The group discussions were my favorite part of the camp. You always walked away with a new perspective of the world. This was only accomplished when people expressed their opinions and learned to disagree. The environment of collaboration and polite disagreement is the very essence of philosophy camp.

Perhaps the most surprising part of philosophy camp was how it changed me as a person. Before, I was a nerdy girl who secretly longed to be accepted by her peers. I struggled to take pride in being a loner, an individual. I wanted to be heard. Going to philosophy camp allowed me to meet other kids who were, in a way, like me.

Realizing you are not alone restores the confidence in who you are. I remember sitting at camp, feeling completely comfortable discussing my opinions on a topic. Then, someone would constructively disagree with me and I had to defend my stance. Sometimes my argument convinced the other, and sometimes I was introduced to a new perspective. This repetitive process taught me how to have a voice.

I kept coming back to philosophy camp, each time becoming a stronger person. Now, I declare myself weird, strange and proudly wear the title of "nerd." Finding your voice is hard, but learning how to use it, is even harder. Asking questions challenges us as thinkers, teachers and students. Curiosity is the foundation of philosophy, and philosophy is the quest of understanding why.

Philosophy Camp Skits

E. Grace Sorensen, Camper
High Class of 2023

For the past two summers, I attended the weeklong Aggie School of Athens philosophy camp at Texas A&M University and during both weeks we were asked to separate into groups and to write skits over the discussions that occurred during the week. Beginning on the first day, each group would spend the last hour of each camp day working on a skit. Then, on the last day of camp, they perform the skits for the leaders of the camp, the rest of the campers, and their parents. I feel that these skits are a great idea. Asking campers to create skits that demonstrate one of the concepts discussed allows them to work together and apply what they have learned over the course of the camp.

Throughout the week, campers have to cooperate within their groups in order to plan, practice, and perform a skit, building teamwork skills and a sense of community. In the beginning of the project, students must come to an agreement over the discussion topic for the skit. If they do disagree, they can find a common point on which they agree or can form the skit around their differences and make it a debate between the two sides and defend their respective points of view. Either way, this helps others to gain a better understanding of the concept and shows how campers interpret camp readings and discussions.

As groups develop the skits, campers work together so that they can finish in time. If they spend all of their time arguing, they will not be able to write a script and practice it before the final day. They will need to cooperate with each other in order to merge their ideas to create a fun and informative skit. Equally important, while working together, students might even make friends. By building these relationships, they have others with whom to discuss philosophy after camp ends, creating their own learning communities.

In addition to teamwork, these skits also act as an opportunity for campers to show that they understand the readings and discussions and to exhibit their application to real-life situations. They need to apply the concepts learned throughout the week, allowing those running the camp to see how students interpret the materials and which discussions interest campers the most. For example, one year, in a discussion on the idea that "seeing is believing," we brought up the idea of flat-earthers believing that the Earth is flat even when presented with evidence to the contrary.

At the end of camp, one group created a skit about the flat-earthers not believing satellite images, demonstrating how some people refuse to accept facts that go against their beliefs. In practice, these skits allow those involved with the camp to see different interpretations of the same idea—much like a discussion. For instance, two groups may create skits over the same concept but may take different stands on the idea.

These groups may disagree over the notion "seeing is believing." One group might create a skit poking fun at those who do not believe what they see; however, the other may bring up instances where no one can be sure about what they are seeing, such as optical illusions. These two skits would show the audience different interpretations of the same idea, providing a useful learning experience for everyone.

Through this skit activity, campers can become more familiar with their fellow campers as well as demonstrate their newfound ideas. They are able to develop their teamwork skills by working together and may even make some friends along the way. Additionally, campers can build critical thinking skills as they plan and perform. Moreover, the leaders of the camp can see if campers understand the material and can apply it to the real world. Ultimately, these skits allow campers to express their thinking in fun, constructive, and educational ways.

Building Confidence, Seeing the Gray, Accepting Other Perspectives

Alina Sorescu (Parent) and Sorin Sorescu (Parent)
with Andrew Sorescu (Camper)

Our son, Andrew, has participated in the philosophy camp every year since it started. We are sure that in the beginning he decided to attend this camp mostly out of curiosity, because philosophy is something that is sadly not covered in the school curriculum. But Andrew soon learned that philosophy is an important discipline that can help him develop as a human being just as much, if not more than other subjects covered in school; as a result, he chose to return twice to the camp.

We had many conversations with him about the philosophy camp. Perhaps the most important lesson that Andrew has learned from this camp is that most issues that humans grapple with are rarely black and white, and that how you deal with the gray in the middle says a lot about your values and outlook on life. Having the ability to listen to the opinion of others, even if they appear contrary to your beliefs, and having the ability to assess evidence in support of a given stance with as much objectivity as humanly possible is a skill that comes from reflection, understanding of other perspectives, introspection, and compassion.

Andrew has always been an open-minded child, but we noticed that after Philosophy camp he has become even more willing to listen to a point of view analytically and to change his mind if he was wrong or if he made a decision based on insufficient information. This is a valuable gift that he received through the group conversations orchestrated at the camp.

Andrew also shared that the philosophy camp helped increase his confidence in his ability to sustain a conversation about deeper topics than the ones typically tackled by thirteen- and fourteen-year-old kids. He told us that in the beginning he found it a bit intimidating to share his opinions in a group setting, but soon he found that by doing so he can learn how to better articulate his thoughts and he can have more meaningful exchanges with his peers. From my vantage point as a parent, I was thrilled to hear him talk in the back of the car with his friends, as I was driving them home after camp, about topics ranging from communism to spirituality, a welcome change from their relatively more superficial conversations about games, sports, or their friends.

In sum, the philosophy camp has played an invaluable role in helping our son develop into a deeper thinker, a more open-minded person, one capable of having deeper relationships and conversations. We also believe that understanding the history of human thought, and how it evolved along the progress of science and the evolution of human spirituality is an essential part of every young person's education.

The omission of philosophy from the curriculum of Texas schools is doing a big disservice to young Texans' ability to think critically, to be more accepting of other people's opinions, and to have a better understanding of the origin of classical schools of thought and religious doctrines. The philosophy camp has been very successful in filling this void for the young people who were fortunate enough to attend it. We can only hope that it will continue to provide value to young people in our community and beyond and we remain very grateful to the efforts of Dr. Katz and her students and staff who have poured their hearts into offering an enriching and exciting opportunity to our children.

The Impact of Philosophy Camp

Surya Sunkari, Camper

I first joined philosophy camp at The Texas A&M University Campus in 2016 when I was eleven years old. This was also the year the camp originally began, and it was remarkably well organized and thought out. It was almost like the organizers were kids and knew exactly what time the campers would be hungry for snacks, interesting topics to talk about, and fun games to play. Philosophy camp has influenced me in so many ways. To name two, it has changed my view on what philosophy is and it has improved my speaking skills with peers.

My original idea of philosophy was just thinking about boring topics and trying to make something out of it. Things like, "What came first? The chicken, or the egg?" are the topics I thought were debated by philosophers. However, going through this camp, I realized that all societies actually need philosophy. It can govern ethics, determine right or wrong, or just make people wiser than they were before. There were many serious discussions that we campers had, along with some lighthearted and funny ones as well; showing us a different side of philosophy. Now, I know that philosophy isn't just finding the answer to life or the chicken and egg problem. It is the activity people use to find truth in relationships, activities, and people.

Another way philosophy camp impacted me is to improve my speaking skills. Being able to share one's opinion and build off of others' opinions is a valuable life skill. Campers unknowingly learn this skill through the interesting group discussions which compel them to share their thoughts about the subject, or even contradict someone else's opinion. This has also improved my leadership skills while dealing with group members at school, trying to come up with ideas for various projects.

This past summer (2019) was my fourth year in philosophy camp, and I very much hope it is not the last. I have made many friends over the past couple of years, and I also want to make new friends in the upcoming camps. Philosophy camp gives me something useful to do over the summer, and if I spent the time at home, I would probably be playing games or wasting time. This camp has influenced me in many ways, and I definitely want to be a part of it for years to come.

IOWA LYCEUM, UNIVERSITY OF IOWA DEPARTMENT OF PHILOSOPHY

Nicholas C. Peters, Camper
Philosophy Major, University of St. Thomas (MN), 2021

Philosophy, as I would come to realize, is everywhere. It was the engine which generally propelled many of the disciplines that we specialize in today. Philosophy is inescapable, but I say this in retrospect. At the time when I first learned about philosophy in an academic setting, I could not nor wished not to connect the dots between the grand questions that philosophers speculated on and the real-life applications.

I always saw philosophy as something abstract. This was something I really enjoyed about the discipline, but also one of the harder things for a fifteen year old to wrap their mind around. At the time when I was doing the philosophy camp at Iowa Lyceum, life for me was getting more concrete. I was learning how to drive, I was starting to work to earn some disposable income, I had started to find girls more interesting, you get the gist. My place in the world had changed from the dreamy, imaginative kid who liked abstract space to someone who felt more materially grounded in their growing individuality. As such, philosophy, as I first encountered it, was simply boring. I didn't look at the clock in the classroom and ponder time, rather I pondered how much time before I would be released.

A year later, I took another course in philosophy, an online class called the *Introduction to Philosophy Through Film*. By this time, I had grown a little more open to philosophy, but there was still something holding me back from truly enjoying it. Speaking in retrospect once more, I believe that I didn't see the "end" of doing philosophy.

It wasn't until I reached college where and when philosophy truly revealed itself to me, and me to it. I am now pursuing my undergraduate degree in philosophy and couldn't be more content with my choice. After bouncing around other disciplines, I realized that the structure of most could be explained by one. I also learned that doing philosophy was an end in itself, and I could do it anywhere. When people ask what I am going to do with a philosophy degree, I can't help but smile, shrug, and tell them to ask me a better question.

Overall, I believe that my father and I would agree that engaging in philosophy is something worthwhile and worth doing. Early exposure to philosophy is crucial to finding not only your place in the world, but the world in your place. While I didn't truly appreciate my time in philosophy camps in my youth, I think that the courses helped me understand concepts that reoccur as I journey forward in life.

We all, at some point or another, ponder philosophical questions, regardless of whether there is structure to these thoughts or not. Yet the framework and tools you can gain from camps which seek to explore deep insights and a way to express them through a civil rhetoric is a more useful guide to understanding these questions, and getting to the end of a logical discussion while enjoying it along the way.

Maeve Ward, Camper

In all honesty, the first time I attended the Lyceum, I didn't even want to go. My mom was determined that I should do something with my summer and signed me up, despite my protestations. It was the beginning of the end. The Lyceum has not been wholly to blame for my current studies. I have been interested in the classical world and religion since Percy Jackson. But it is at least partially liable for turning me into the humanities monster I have become.

Before my time in the Lyceum, I viewed philosophy as an it's-all-been-done sort of discipline- an area of study meant for the smart people of the liberal arts who were kind of out of touch. Musty. My introduction to philosophy through the Lyceum was possibly the best-case scenario to turn that around. As corny as it sounds, I realized that philosophy isn't a noun, but a verb. 'Twas I who was the philosopher! Rather than old professors writing facts on boards, the Lyceum was fun and engaging. The pedagogy- notably the Monty Python "Argument" skit and increasingly complex trolley problems- was accessible and inviting, though I still don't know how to define a sandwich or why tomato soup is excluded from the category of punch.

Even if a conclusion isn't new to the world, the sensation of coming to it can be new to the individual. My education up until the Lyceum had consisted mostly of being told conclusions drawn by other people. Of course, I had been taught critical thinking already, but I had never really been asked to use it. All the most memorable moments of my education orbit around the internal experience of thought invention, an experience I frequently had during the Lyceum. As I am beginning to learn, the idea that true knowledge can only be acquired through experience is a theme that is common among different religions. That I learned this fact in the Lyceum—as I did with much of this kind of learning—has been very impactful.

My participation gave me quite a bit of intellectual confidence. Often it can be difficult, especially for younger students, to have the confidence to interrogate the ideas of their intellectual "superiors." It is a practice I still struggle with as a college student. Now, research projects where I get to dialogue with other scholars and ultimately argue my own perspective are my favorite assignments, and the feeling of synthesizing information into an argument has become a hunger impossible to satiate. By allowing us to discuss and argue, the Lyceum forced us to question each other's arguments.

I am now majoring in classical studies and religion. I have found that it can often be difficult for modern audiences to humanize historical figures—for example, the characterization of the figures portrayed in Hamilton. Cicero, too, is often a slam dunk to clown on. My interest in the classical world and in religion is to empathize with and understand these people's lives. Yes, we can make fun of Cicero's long-windedness, or we can snicker along with Diogenes as he ridicules Plato, but philosophy is an attempt to understand and contextualize the self in a world that doesn't make sense. For me, what started out as a mental jungle gym has transformed into a tool that I use every day for myself academically and in essentially every other aspect of my life. I surely would have had a turn with philosophy without the Lyceum, but the taste for critical thinking I got from it gave me a jump start into really becoming an independent thinker.

Christopher C. Peters, MD, Parent

My love of philosophy came later in life. During college, I largely sleep-walked through two semesters of Western Civilization, earning middling grades. I started out in architecture, ended up getting a degree in psychology, and in the process discovered a love and knack for the "hard sciences." I went on to medical school, then two surgical residencies. By that time, I was focused on my growing family and building my surgical career.

Beginning in 2007, during the buildup to the financial crisis, I began a self-guided study of economics. That in turn led to explorations into behavioral economics, game theory, political philosophy, rhetoric, and complexity science. I was excited to have discovered a whole range of human thought, some old and some new, which I had previously largely ignored.

I tried to share my newfound excitement with my wife and three sons. Sometimes they shared my interest, but more often they probably just humored me. Undaunted, I looked for opportunities to share these exciting worlds of human thought going back centuries, yet still expanding in the modern era.

In 2014, our two eldest sons, Cole and Jake, attended a weeklong summer philosophy camp at the University of Iowa campus, called the Iowa Lyceum. Cole was an rising junior in high school, and Jake would be a high school sophomore. The following spring, both earned three hours of college credit for an *Introduction to Philosophy Through Film* class through the University of Iowa. Our youngest son, Caleb, also attended the Iowa Lyceum in 2018, prior to his junior year of high school.

I would like to say that these experiences were immediately transformative, but that wouldn't be honest. While I believe all of our sons gained valuable new insights from their summer experiences, I think they somewhat resented me for taking away part of their summer breaks! But, while not immediately transformative, I do think those experiences have had lasting effects.

Caleb is now a senior in high school, has gained a great appreciation for aesthetics, and will begin a degree in architecture next year. Jake has since become a father himself, and I am regularly amazed by his wonderfully loving parental skills and a growing maturity which is far beyond what I possessed at his age. Cole is in his last year of college, majoring in, of all things, philosophy! I have greatly enjoyed talking with him about his studies, his new insights, and am truly excited for his future.

MOSHI WINTER CAMP

Su-Yin Bouchot

What comes to mind when you hear the word *Moshi*? What does that mean? Is it even an actual word? Maybe not, but I know that Moshi Moustache is an amazing philosophy program founded by Caroline Murgue. In February 2018, Moshi Moustache held a winter camp for children to learn about philosophy and the impact it has on our lives. I attended the camp with several other children from five to ten years old. The winter camp was very educational. All of us walked out with a smile and something new that we had learned.

One topic that was focused on was *community*. We learned that community can take on several meanings. For instance, it can represent the relationships between friends, family, and others. A community could also refer to a group of people living in the same area, like my New York neighborhood, Long Island City. It can also mean working together. During the camp, we did many activities to bring the word "community" to life. My favorite was when we made clay animals and learned how to film a StopMotion video. We worked as a group and wrote the script to film the clay animals working together to build their new community.

What I learned during camp helped me better understand the importance of *community* and why it is beneficial to our everyday lives. For example, when I was living in Long Island City, we had a park cleanup day where anybody could volunteer to help clean up our parks so everyone can enjoy them. I was very happy to take part in the cleanup as I felt I helped contribute to the community and the neighborhood I love. Now that I am living in Hong Kong, my participation in the school community has helped me make new friends and adjust to my new life quicker. If everybody plays their role as a part of their community, I believe we will all build better relationships with the people around us and live happier lives.

PACT—OHIO STATE

Ezra Johnson, PACT Camper 2017–2018

My interest in philosophy began when I received an e-mail about a new summer camp opening up at OSU. I would spend one week learning about rights and liberty through debates, texts, and movies. There were also more social activities in the program to allow the kids to interact more informally. This sounded like a blast considering I had no other plans for the summer, and I liked the idea of challenging myself with something new. I completed the application and signed up.

The camp was different from any type of classroom setting that I had ever been a part of. Besides the faster pace, it had much more subjective and interesting material than what I typically would have covered at school. Most days, we had the opportunity to listen to philosophy professors introduce different topics and then make our own judgments and opinions about them. It was the fact that the same lecture could create such diverse responses that made me want to keep philosophy in my life. My favorite activity we did was in my second year at the camp when we used a 3D graphics system and each got to experience the trolley problem in a more immersive way. It was fascinating how many justifications there could be for both decisions even when everyone was given the same scenario.

Overall, I really enjoyed the chance to speak with other teens who had the ability to discuss things that didn't have clear answers in such a collaborative environment. Philosophy is certain to be in my life as I continue to learn; however, this may not be as a profession or major. The most important takeaways from my experience at camp were the critical thinking skills I gained by forming arguments. I will always be grateful for those skills.

Larada McCreary, PACT Camper 2017–2018

I have always had a deep-rooted passion for words. This said, passion is what transformed the little girl who always aced her spelling test in grade school into a full-fledged poet in her adolescent years. I have also always been interested in social justice and had my heart set on becoming a civil rights attorney when I grew up. It wasn't until I discovered a flyer for the Philosophy and Critical Thinking (PACT) summer camp at OSU back in 2017 (my junior year in high school) that I developed an interest in philosophy. When I attended the first session of PACT summer camp, I fell in love with philosophy immediately. It was almost as if it was my calling and I had found exactly what I wanted to do for the rest of my life. The friendships and bonds that I built were also a major plus too; I still keep in contact with many of the fellow participants who were in my cohorts both years (2017–2018).

I attended the following year when I was an incoming freshman at OSU. The following week I changed my major from English to philosophy because I became so passionate about it. I could not imagine myself pursuing field other than philosophy. Even now as I am wrapping up my first year at OSU,

I have on numerous occasions found myself utilizing some of the skills I developed at the PACT summer camp and applying them to particular assignments and discussions. The ways in which we analyzed and built on theories around social justice and what it means to varying degrees was sort of electrifying. I had not realized that there were so many ways to ask and answer questions in philosophy and it was the lesson that kept me wanting more. I had never thought about social justice or even rights in a philosophical context until I attended the PACT summer camp. That experience has helped me by enabling my passions for social justice and philosophy to come together.

I speak not only for myself but also for other members of PACT 2018 Session 1 when I say that the PACT summer camp helped me tap into potential that I was not even aware existed within my abilities as a critical thinker. Many people wouldn't necessarily perceive the ability to think critically and analytically as a talent or vital skill, but I found during my time with the PACT summer camp that it is. The instructors did an impeccable job instructing the lessons and it was evident that they were very thought out and put together. They found a way to make something informative into something fun and that alone was one of my greatest highlights from the camp.

The PACT summer camp truly nurtures young critical and analytical thinkers and cultivates them into young philosophers. I highly recommend anyone who knows a high schooler with a gift for those two things to push them to attend this camp. I have a younger sister who will be attending one of the sessions this summer and she is extremely excited because I have done nothing but rave about my experience. I look forward to her sharing those experiences with me. I am also excited to see what is in store for all of the future cohorts because I am certain that whatever they do, it will be fantastic. All in all, the PACT summer camp at OSU is guaranteed to be a worthwhile, intellectual experience that is bound to enhance a young critical thinker's abilities and skill sets.

Shefali Sinha, PACT Camper 2018

I vividly remember seeing the flyer for this camp show up in my e-mail. At first, I was hesitant about applying. It seemed like the concept of "justice" was too large for my brain to grasp. "If I can't even define justice, then how am I going to be able to discuss it?," I remember thinking. I signed up, not expecting much. When I got accepted, I felt a wave of hesitance flow through me. However, I knew that I would learn so much if I went. And so, I did. And I am glad I went. This camp was so memorable. The campers all bonded together so well over serious discussions, fake acting scenarios, and silly jokes. Those warm summer days as we researched for our debates, learned about injustice and justice through paradoxes, and discussed severe issues are some of my favorite memories.

This camp helped me think about problems in a new way. We, as human beings, have natural lenses, or biases, that we look through. This warps our view of the world. Yet, philosophy is such a powerful force which rips those lenses off. At first, we stumble around blinded as everything we thought we knew turns out wrong. However, philosophy lends us a guiding hand and supports us in traveling in this new world and helps us notices unique nuances along the way. I have can see this in my own high school experience. My thinking has matured so much, and I am now able to look at problems, small and global, in an unbiased and untainted way. It is refreshing to know that I can work out problems using my knowledge in philosophy without feeling lost.

However, philosophy is such a big topic. I have learned about 1 percent of philosophy. Philosophy is so important, and I have noticed that I am typically reading books and articles, listening to speeches, and naturally thinking about philosophy. It is so crucial for people, especially students, to learn about philosophy. It helps us grow up a little mentally, which can help us in high school and college. It helps us unravel complex issues and injustices in the world while providing us with an identity. As a result, I am planning on taking at least one philosophy course in college. It is a course that can benefit everyone and every major.

Kevin and Melissa Shoultz, PACT Parents 2017–2018

My husband and I cannot say enough good things about the PACT camp offered at Ohio State each summer! Our son, Michael, has attended the last two years and absolutely loves it. He comes home each day energized and excited by his interaction with the staff and his peers.

Michael first heard about the program through his high school's guidance office and was intrigued because of a recently discovered interest in philosophy. At the time, he did not have much knowledge on the subject but had a clear affinity for it. However, after going to the camp his first year, he gained a solid foundation of understanding of the subject that led him to a much deeper interest. He began to do much more independent research and study of philosophy, largely through authors and resources recommended to him at the camp. He was reading everything he could get his hands on!

Michael's second year attending was quite similar. He found the camp to be just as enjoyable and intellectually stimulating. When we asked him his overall thoughts on the program he admits that both years he found that the interaction with his peers was a somewhat surprising realization. Prior to this, there had not been many opportunities for him to discuss philosophical topics, to the depth he was able to, with students of similar age. He found this common respect for intellectualism in the discipline of philosophy to be encouraging. Quite frankly, he thrived in this setting!

He has only great things to say about the program itself, the topics discussed, and the experience of spending his days on the Ohio State campus. As for the staff, they are a fantastic group of intelligent and engaging educators and he absolutely loved his interaction with them! We still hear (a year later) "When Jamie and I were discussing . . ." Or "Lavender agrees that . . ." He seriously admires, and appreciated his time with, this particular group and as his parents, we appreciate his boosted self-esteem, newfound confidence and seeing his passion for learning encouraged by this experience and staff. We are also extremely grateful for the scholarship opportunities offered by the program. We were encouraged to apply and are so thankful that we did!

In closing, not only was this program a fun way to spend a few weeks in the summers of his freshman and sophomore years of high school, but it led to his becoming more actively engaged in his education. He started taking advantage of Ohio's College Credit Plus program as a sophomore and has been attending college classes throughout his high school experience. In fact, he will actually be graduating high school with his Associates degree completed at the same time. As a rising high school senior, we are all very excited to see HIM so excited about his upcoming college years and the journey he is about to embark on and it all started the summer he was thirteen years and discovered PACT at OSU!

SALISBURY UNIVERSITY (SU) SUMMER CAMP

Philosophy Summer Camp Review
Sophia Smith

How long does it take to know oneself? This was one of the many intriguing and thought-provoking questions that we discussed in Sapere Aude, the philosophy summer camp for high school students at Salisbury University (SU). Sapere Aude, a Latin phrase considered the motto of enlightenment, means "dare to use your own reason," which is precisely what we did.

During this five-day experience, we not only learned about the origins and history of philosophy and deep-thinking, but also explored difficult moral and ethical dilemmas. This experience challenged not only what we, as teenagers, *thought* we knew, but also our perceptions of ourselves and the world around us.

Imagine that you are walking near a train track when you see five people tied to the rails, and you can hear the train quickly coming toward them. You notice a signal lever that would reroute the train down a side-track if you pulled it, saving the five people—but killing one person, who is tied to the alternative rails. Would you pull the lever? Most of us, including myself, immediately said yes, because we thought that saving five people and sacrificing only one was obviously the ethically correct choice—or was it?

It was pointed out that by not pulling the lever, you are not killing anyone. You are simply just a bystander, at the wrong place and the wrong time. But by pulling the lever, you are consciously making the decision to kill that one person, regardless of whether or not you are saving the five—you still killed one. Who are you to act like a higher power? Who are you to interfere with fate? Who are you to decide who lives, and who dies?

If you did not pull the lever, those affected would extend beyond those five people—their deaths would trigger a ripple effect, causing their friends, families and loved ones a great deal of grief and pain. The five individual's deaths would affect far more people than just the one individual's death would. But then again, would that ripple affect really even be your fault? Or would it be at the fault of fate? It truly is a never-ending circle of question, and many people, including me, had their perspectives changed about what was *actually* the moral choice, and completely changed their minds about what they would do.

As we participated in these kinds of debates and deep conversations, we improved our abilities to solve problems, expanded our boundaries of knowledge, learned how to apply these concepts to our everyday lives, and had fun in the process. We did lots of outdoor collaborative games, activities, and arts and crafts, such as decorating rocks and tie-dyeing T-shirts. There were several SU students who helped out as teaching fellows and developed our academic and writing skills, giving us an idea of what it meant to study philosophy at the college-level. They acted as mentors and were very open and receptive to listening to our thoughts and sharing ideas with us, and I became very close with several of them.

In the academic lectures, we learned about the roots of philosophy, such Plato's and Socrates's theories of the soul, and questioned the concepts of emotions, knowledge, consent, identity, and race. We examined pop cultural artifacts, like songs we hear on the radio, and analyzed them with these ideas in mind to find deeper meanings.

We also had the opportunity to attend a special event at the Chipman Cultural Center, where we got to meet two famous writers, Marc Aronson and A. J. Verdelle. They each spoke to us about their journeys as writers as we asked them questions and held small-group breakout sessions. After the event, a book truck with dozens of free books was parked outside.

We learned that the House of SpeakEasy book truck, from New York City, travels throughout the country to provide free books to readers in areas that they consider to be "book deserts." I got to pick out as many books as I wanted as I spoke to the people who coordinated the truck and listened to their many engaging stories of their times on the road. Talking with the authors was especially exciting for me personally as an aspiring writer, and having access to their creative processes was very special to me.

All in all, Sapere Aude philosophy summer camp was an experience that will always stay with me. From the captivating origins of philosophy, to the supportive teaching fellows, to the cool projects and games, to the real-world applications, and to the new friends I met, I had the best week ever and I highly recommend it to any high schooler that wants to have fun while learning more about the marvels of philosophy.

Philosophy Camp 2019: Sapere Aude

Ryan Cadwaller

Brimming with deep thought and the constant circulation of new ideas and perspectives, the environment created in the Philosophy Summer Camp at Salisbury University was unmatched by any conventional classroom. Critical thinking was not a mere abstract idea, but the foundation for every conversation that sprang to life among the flurry of insights. Born from a question proposed by a lecture at the beginning of the day, each conversation was driven by the never-ending "why" that seemed to be the immediate response to every idea proposed by campers and teaching fellows alike.

These conversations were built upon deep analysis and thorough questioning of every thought tossed into the circle. Because of this, we were forced to think about life and the world around us in new ways. Because each lecture was followed immediately by an open discussion, the balance between learning and free conversation was maintained perfectly as we challenged each other's thoughts and worked, as a group, toward a common agreement.

Discussions during the camp encouraged a unique style of teamwork, where individual opposing ideas are used to move the entire group toward a common destination of "the right answer." It was rare that a group consensus would be reached, but that was never a complication. The value of every conversation at the camp was in the discussion itself, not the answer to the original question. "Is race real?," "Do computers have minds?," "What is philosophy?" where all among the inquiries proposed. Looking back on these questions, I still cannot come up with a yes or no answer, but that only proves the worth of the camp.

Our group discussions about race, computers, trains, maps, caves, shadows, and even the soul never became argumentative or polarizing, despite them coming from what were technically "yes" or "no" questions. In life, there is always more to be heard. People tend to turn a blind eye to new ideas or perspectives, especially when someone is accustomed to their own particular viewpoint. The atmosphere of the camp, one in which every person is excited to hear from others and gain new insights, was something that made the camp feel so different than any classroom or camp that I had ever been in.

Philosophy, as a whole, is underappreciated and even overlooked when it is seen simply as a course to be taught, lumped into the same category as history, psychology, or literature. Philosophy holds the potential to be so much more meaningful. Philosophy is a combination of all these fields, binding facts and knowledge together with ideas and opinions. The Philosophy Summer Camp for High School Students at SU is a perfect way to introduce students into the endlessly engaging world of philosophy, teaching the value of learning though inquiry, and most importantly, daring to use our own reason.

NOTES

1. This is an updated and expanded version of the essay originally published in *Growing Up with Philosophy Camp: How Thinking Develops Friendship, Community, and a Sense of Self* (Lanham, MD: Rowman & Littlefield, 2020).

2. http://platosallegory.com/.

Appendix: Precollege Philosophy Works

Meta-Analysis of the Effectiveness of Philosophy for Children Program on Students' Cognitive Outcomes (Excerpt)[1]

Sijin Yan, Lynne Masel Walters, Zhuoying Wang, and Dr. Chia-Chiang Wang

Philosophy for Children (often abbreviated as P4C) is an educational program that provides students in K–12 settings opportunities to engage in communities of philosophical inquiry with the long-term aim of improving their cognitive abilities (Lam, 2012; Trickey & Topping, 2004). The evaluation of P4C as an educational movement concerns its impact on students according to different metrics and also provides insights on various ways this program can be implemented in school districts to benefit more student, especially those who are challenged and disadvantaged, at an affordable cost (Gorard, Siddiqui, & Huat see, 2015). Since the 1970s, evaluative, empirical research in P4C can be divided briefly into two categories: (1) cognitive outcomes and (2) sociopsychological outcomes related to attitudes toward academics, prosocial attitudes and behavior. This meta-analysis will be solely focused on P4C's impact on students' cognitive abilities.

In 2004 and 2005, two systematic reviews (García-Moriyón et al., 2005; Trickey & Topping, 2004) were conducted to synthesize research on the effectiveness of P4C. First, the quantitative systematic analysis by Trickey and Topping (2004) investigated the influence of P4C on students in general, with the conclusion that P4C has a moderate positive effect on students' abilities with low variance. It collected eight controlled experiments regarding P4C from 1970s to 2002. Even though the relationship between the two has not been yet been accepted by researchers (Hidi, Renninger, & Krapp, 2004), they combined the cognitive outcomes and affective abilities without a theoretical foundation for doing so. The second study is a meta-analysis conducted by García-Moriyón, Rebollo, and Colom (2005), in which they examined the relationship between P4C and reasoning skills as outlined in eighteen studies published from 1976 to 2002, with the finding that P4C has a positive moderate influence on students' reasoning abilities. This meta-analysis included eighteen experiments. The results showed significant differences among posttest experiments, single group studies with pre- and posttest, and controlled experiments, in which the more rigorous controlled experiments tended to show lower effect sizes.

These two reviews (García-Moriyón et al., 2005; Trickey & Topping, 2004) provided significant contributions in understanding the impacts of implementing P4C in K–12 education. However, a new meta-analysis is needed to address the following issues in the contemporary situation.

First, after the publication of the two earlier meta-analyses, a larger collection of literature on the effects of P4C on cognitive outcomes has been generated with an increasing rigor of study designs, a larger number of participants, and follow-up studies (Fair et al., 2015a; Fair et al., 2015b; Topping & Trickey, 2007a, 2007b). Thus, researchers now have the opportunity to improve the rigor of a systematic analysis by only including studies with random controlled experiments or quasi-experiments and analyze these findings in detail through moderator analyses to find if the relationship between cognitive outcomes and P4C intervention is depended upon other variables such as duration of the program, sample size, and so forth.

Second, since the P4C movement has spread worldwide and research was conducted on different continents (Lam, 2012; Marashi, 2008; Nia, 2014; Youssef, 2014), a meta-analysis at this stage can involve an exhaustive search globally in English and capture the multiplicity of P4C practices worldwide. Thus, the present study aims at conducting a more recent and detailed analysis of the literature to help educators acquire a clearer understanding of the effectiveness of P4C movement as a globalized phenomenon.

The purpose of the current meta-analysis is to examine the reported effectiveness of P4C from 2002 to 2016, immediately following the publication of the two articles that analyzed studies from 1970s to 2002. In addition, this meta-analysis examines which variables—participant age, socioeconomic status, study location, assessment measure, duration—of the intervention might moderate the magnitude of the aggregated effect sizes. The following are our research questions:

- What does the cumulative research suggest regarding the overall effectiveness of P4C on students' cognitive abilities?
- Do study design, students' backgrounds (grade level and socioeconomic status), location and duration of intervention, characteristics of cognitive outcome measurements influence the magnitude of the effect size of included studies?

METHODOLOGY

In this study, the effectiveness of P4C was tested through a meta-analysis, which is a quantitative systematic review that merges the results of many independent researchers, conducted on a particular topic and performs statistical analysis (Çoğaltay & Karadağ, 2016).

This study searched referred published journals and doctoral dissertations through online databases, nonelectronic journal search of the journal *Thinking: Philosophy for Children*, and the Google scholar search engine. In order to be included in this meta-analysis, studies had to meet the following criteria. First, the population of interest was precollegiate students enrolled in a P4C program and their control-group counterparts. College studies and teacher education research were excluded from the study. Second, all the included studies must have explicit pedagogical markers of "community of (philosophical) inquiry" that shares the common practices of providing stimulus (stories, questions, pictures, or other media), students' questioning, and building on each other's ideas. Third, the retrieved study should be published between 2002 and 2016 in a *refereed journal* or as a thesis/dissertation. Fourth, the study must be either random controlled experiments or quasi-experiments, using quantitative measure of outcomes to calculate the effect sizes of the intervention, with outcome variables that contained a measurement of cognitive outcomes, such as reasoning ability, comprehension ability, general cognitive ability, and academic development. Also, this meta-analysis focused on comparing the cognitive outcomes of P4C as the experimental group with other control groups where participants did not receive any thinking skill intervention. Thus, studies that did not contain a control group were excluded.

Then, a coding process was conducted, which is a data extraction process, picking clear and appropriate data from the pile of complex information (Çoğaltay & Karadağ, 2016). After the coding manual was created, two coders (both of whom are coauthors in this paper) initially met to go over the coding manual until consensus was achieved. To determine interrater reliability, the two researchers independently coded five studies (31.25% of the sixteen articles). The interrater reliability was 90.0 percent across those studies. Analysis of coder disagreements resulted in the refinement of some definitions and decision rules for some codes. Then, each coder individually coded the remainder of the studies. During the coding process, the first coder contacted the original authors from two different references for standard deviations and means to calculate the effect sizes. One set of data was obtained and another contact for data was not successful. After a more thorough reading and coding of the extant papers, researchers excluded another six articles that were not aligned with the inclusion criteria.

Effect size computation, test of homogeneity, and moderator analysis were conducted in the stage of data analysis. Cohen's *d* was used to adjust and determine the effect sizes of each study. All the effect sizes in each study were aggregated to one effect size as the cognitive outcome. All data analyses involving effect sizes were weighted analysis. Two main models, namely fixed effects model and random effects model, were utilized in the analysis of heterogeneous distribution of effect sizes.

RESULTS AND DISCUSSION

A total of ten controlled experiments were included in this analysis, which together report the findings of eight independent studies and two follow-up studies. Table A.1 provides an overview of the characteristics of each citation included in the synthesis. Table A.2 provides the overall results and omnibus test of this meta-analysis. The overall effect size aggregated from the ten studies was 0.43 with a 95 percent confidence interval, ranging from

Appendix: Precollege Philosophy Works   185

Table A.1 Characteristics of Included Studies

Reference	Study Type	Location	Sample Size	Grade/Age Level	Outcome Measure	Effect Size	Variance
(Abbasi & Ajam, 2016)	Intervention	Iran	50	Second	Questionnaire of Educational Progress*	0.870	0.080
(Fair et al., 2015b)	Intervention	United States	177	Seventh	CogAT	0.590	0.020
(Fair et al., 2015a)	Follow-Up	United States	115	Seventh Grade—Two Years after	CogAT	0.570	0.030
(Lam, 2012)	Intervention	China	28	Secondary School First Grade	NJTRS	0.590	0.190
(Marashi, 2008)	Intervention	Iran	60	Eighth	NJTRS	1.100	0.070
(Naderi, 2014)	Intervention	Iran	60	High School First Grade	Abedi's Test of Creativity	1.190	0.070
(Tok & Mazı, 2015)	Intervention	Turkey	74	Fifth Grade	Reading Comprehension Test* and Listening Comprehension Test*	0.162	0.035
(Topping & Trickey, 2007a)	Intervention	United Kingdom	540	Ten-year-old students	CAT	0.25	0.01
(Topping & Trickey, 2007b)	Follow-Up	United Kingdom	183	Ten-Year-Old Students (Two Years After)	CAT	0.400	0.020
(Youssef, 2014)	Intervention	Australia	222	Sixth Grade	Reading Comprehension Test	0.340	0.020

Note: CogAT: Cognitive Ability Test (American Version); CAT: Cognitive Ability Test (United Kingdom Version); NJTRS: New Jersey Test of Reasoning Skills; *: Tests developed by researchers.

Table A.2 Overall Results and Omnibus Test of P4C Studies

	k	N	Median ES (d)	Fixed Effect ES (d)	Fixed Effect 95% CI	Random Effect ES (d)	Random Effect 95% CI	Q
P4C	10	1,509	.58	.43	[.33, .53]	.50	[.33, .66]	26.59**

Note: k = study size; N = total number of participants; CI = confidence interval; Q = omnibus test of homogeneity.
** p < .01.

0.33 to 0.53. According to Cohen's Rule of Thumb (VanVoorhis & Morgan, 2007), the mean effect size represents that P4C has a moderate, positive overall cognitive effect for students who are in second to tenth grade.

According to the findings of this meta-analysis, the P4C program has shown a moderate, positive influence on students' cognitive outcomes. This result corroborates the previous literature on the program that states that P4C has a positive impact on students' various types of cognitive abilities (Fair et al., 2015a; Fair et al., 2015b; García-Moriyón et al., 2005; Topping & Trickey, 2007a, 2007b; Trickey & Topping, 2004).

In this study, the homogeneity test was found to be statistically significant ($Q = 26.59$, $p < 0.01$), which means that there is more variability in effect sizes than would be expected from sampling error around the mean. Since the homogeneity test was found to be statistically significant, a moderator analysis was used to find out the potential explanations for variance among effect sizes. In this meta-analysis, subgroup analysis was employed to detect moderating effects. Seven moderator variables were tested: grade level, socioeconomic status of students, location of studies, study design (random or quasi-experiments), total time of intervention, outcome measures, and type of outcomes. Table A.3 provides a detailed statistical description of the result of moderator analysis.

Two of the seven moderators revealed statistically significant effects. They were research location (two subgroups: Asia and Western countries) and type of outcomes (three subgroups: general cognitive ability, reasoning skills and academic achievement). The tests of homogeneity indicated no statistical differences by grade levels, socioeconomic status of participants, methods of group assignments, duration of the intervention, and outcome measures.

P4C and Students' Grade Levels

There was no statistically significant cognitive outcome in the effectiveness of P4C based on the grade levels of students. This result sheds lights on the

Table A.3 The Overall Effectiveness of P4C

Moderator Testing of Study Variable	k	N	d	95% CI	Q_B	ANOVA
Research Location						
Asia	5	272	.69	[.46, .91]		>N-A
Non-Asian Countries	5	1,237	.39	[.27, .51]	5.16*	
Grade at Intervention						
2–5	4	416	.51	[.34, .69]		
6–10	6	1,093	.42	[.29, .55]	0.75	
SES of Participants						
Disadvantaged	4	1,015	.40	[.27, .53]		
Others	6	494	.55	[.37, .72]	1.74	
Methods of Group Assignment						
Random	4	811	.44	[.33, .54]		
Quasi Experiment	6	698	.52	[.38, .66]	0.83	
Total Time of Intervention						
5-20 Hours	4	445	.34	[.18, .51]		
21-30 Hours	3	579	.28	[.13, .43]		
More than 40 Hours	3	427	.47	[.28, .66]	2.41	
Outcome Measure						
CAT or CogAT	4	1,015	.40	[.27, .53]		
Others	6	494	.55	[.37, .72]	1.74	
Type of Outcomes						
General Cognitive Outcomes	4	1,015	.40	[.27, .53]		
Reasoning Skills	2	148	1.06	[.72, 1.40]		> C & R
Reading Comprehension	2	296	.28	[.06, .50]	15.44***	

Note: k = study size; N = number of participants; CI = confidence interval; Q_B = between-groups test of homogeneity; ANOVA = significant result. * $p < .05$, *** $p < .0$.

question regarding P4C and students' age. Philosophy education is traditionally assumed to be appropriate for students no younger than secondary school age (Lipman & Sharp, 1978). But this moderator analysis indicates that both the studies with grade two to five students and the studies with grade six to ten students benefited from P4C program (grade 2–5: $d = 0.51$; grade 6–10: $d = 0.42$). There was no statistically meaningful difference between the aggregated effect sizes of the two subgroups.

During the screening stage of this study, we found a small number of studies (Dasí et al., 2013; Säre et al., 2016) that have practiced P4C with very young children who are below the age of five. Even though this study is exclusively focused on K–12 education, it is worth mentioning that the study conducted by Dasí et al. (2013) showed a clear significant improvement in sociopsychological abilities among the five-year-old children and a partial improvement in the four-year-old children after participating a few sessions of P4C program. Also, one study (Säre et al., 2016) showed that P4C positively influenced preschoolers' verbal reasoning skills. These researches provide information for educators and researchers to understand the unfamiliar area in which young children are involved in rather than excluded from philosophy. Future research can consider examining how P4C affects the cognitive outcome of children in kindergarten or preschool.

P4C and the Socioeconomic Status of Students

In this sample of studies, we used two categories for the socioeconomic status (SES) of the participants. The first group consisted of students who received free-lunch or were classified as "economically disadvantaged" by the local districts. The second group of students is not identified as part of the free-lunch program, or was classified as from middle (or upper) class families. No significant heterogeneity in effect sizes was found between the two groups of students.

P4C and Study Design

To warrant the rigor of this meta-analysis, the authors set up stringent criteria for the inclusion of studies in which only random controlled trials and quasi-experiments were brought in the synthesis. From the moderator analysis, no significant difference was found between effect sizes of random controlled experiments and quasi-experiments which were included in this meta-analysis.

P4C and Duration of Interventions

The authors of this study divided the literature into three subgroups based on the duration of interventions: five to twenty hours ($k = 4$), twenty-one to forty hours ($k = 3$), and more than forty hours ($k = 3$). The result showed that none of the duration levels statistically varied from one another. Thus, there was no noteworthy difference between different levels of duration of intervention in the effectiveness of P4C on students' cognitive outcomes. This was not expected since several studies (Fair et al., 2015a; Fair et al., 2015b; García-Moriyón et al., 2005; Topping & Trickey, 2007a) have proposed that P4C should be implemented for a significant period of time before the program shows results.

That being said, our result resonates with one P4C study (Fair et al., 2015b). In this project, the authors replicated a previous experiment conducted by Topping and Trickey (Topping & Trickey, 2007a), in which they shortened the duration of the P4C intervention to less than half of the former one: from fifty-eight weeks to twenty-two to twenty-six weeks. The result showed that P4C still had a moderate effect on students' general cognitive ability. This suggests that a short time of exposure to P4C may also have a meaningful impact on students' cognitive outcomes.

P4C and Outcome Measure: CAT or Non-CAT

Studies included were examined according to their outcome measures. Four studies using Cognitive Ability Tests were accepted as CAT subgroup; six studies applying other types of outcome measures were accepted as Non-CAT subgroup. No significant heterogeneity was found between these two subgroups.

P4C and Types of Cognitive Outcomes

A significant difference among different types of outcomes was found (Q_B = 15.44, $p < .001$). The studies (Lam, 2012; Marashi, 2008) which tested the improvement of reasoning skills through P4C yielded the largest estimations ($d = 1.06$), which is a large effect size. P4C used in improving general cognitive abilities ($d = 0.40$), which is a moderate effect size. Reading comprehension ability ($d = 0.28$) is a small effect size. This suggests that P4C has significant, positive influence on students' reasoning skills, and moderate effects on general cognitive ability and comprehension ability.

P4C and Locations

This meta-analysis covers five studies conducted in the United Kingdom, Australia, and the United States and five studies in Asian countries—Iran,

Turkey, and China. Through moderator analysis, a significant difference between the two groups was found ($Q = 5.16, p < .05$). The studies in Asian countries had higher effect sizes ($d = 0.69$) than those studies conducted in Western countries ($d = 0.39$). On the first sight, it seems that the globalizing P4C program has generated more positive influences on students' cognitive outcomes in non-Western countries than Western countries. There are several possible accounts for this phenomenon.

First, the studies in Asia at this point tend to have smaller sample sizes. Because P4C is still new to educators and researchers in those countries (Lam, 2012; Marashi, 2008), including Iran, China and Turkey, these studies are often *pilot studies* with small sample sizes. Moreover, since P4C was initiated in the United States in the 1970s (Brandt, 1988), it is a more relatively well-known to the educators in the United States, United Kingdom, Australia, and other Western countries. Thus, studies conducted in these areas tended to evaluate P4C in *large school districts* (Fair et al., 2015b; Toppings & Trickey, 2007a; Youssef, 2014). In this meta-analysis, the mean sample size of Western studies is three times higher than the mean sample size of non-Western studies.

Smaller sample sizes may contribute to the quality of teacher education and P4C implementation. Pedagogically speaking, all the studies have utilized community of inquiry as the core pedagogy. Though it might be the case that there are more experienced practitioners in countries where P4C is more well-known, it is also possible that the reverse is true. This is because the practitioners in pilot studies may have received more focused philosophy education while in studies with large sample size teacher education and motivation for practicing P4C are not easy to control.

Another possible explanation is that several studies in non-Western countries tested the improvement of reasoning skills among students (Lam, 2012; Marashi, 2008; Othman & Hashim, 2006), while no Western research included here specifically examined the reasoning abilities of students. According to the moderator analysis regarding the effect sizes of studies with different types of outcomes, there is a statistically significant difference between reasoning skills and other types of outcomes. If P4C is more effective to the improvement of reasoning skills, then the discrepancy between the effect sizes in Western and non-Western studies is understandable.

Overall, P4C was found to have a moderate, positive overall effect on students' cognitive
Outcomes, with significant impact on reasoning skills: The authors suggest that P4C may be considered as an effective thinking program for teachers in K–12 education. More studies that explore the connection between community of inquiry, philosophical thinking, and the sociopsychological development of children are strongly recommended, including children at a very young age.

NOTE

1. This chapter is an excerpt of longer article, "Meta-Analysis of the Effectiveness of Philosophy for Children Programs on Students' Cognitive Outcomes," by Sijin Yan, Lynne Masel Walters, Zhuoying Wang, and Chia-Chiang Wang originally published in Analytic Teaching and Philosophical Praxis Vol 39/No. 1 (2018).

REFERENCES

Abbasi, Z., & Ajam, A. A. (2016). The Effects of Philosophical Stories on Emotional Intelligence and Educational Progress of Students in Science Lessons. *Mediterranean Journal of Social Sciences, 7*(2), 282.

Brandt, R. (1988). On Philosophy in the Curriculum: A Conversation with Matthew Lipman. *Educational Leadership, 46*(1), 34–37.

Çoğaltay, N., & Karadağ, E. (2016). The Effect of Educational Leadership on Organizational Variables: A Meta–Analysis Study in the Sample of Turkey. *Educational Sciences: Theory & Practice, 16*(2).

Colom, R., Moriyon, F. G., Magro, C., & Morilla, E. (2014). The Long-term Impact of Philosophy for Children: A Longitudinal Study (Preliminary Results). *Analytic Teaching and Philosophical Praxis, 35*(1).

Dasí, M. G., Quintanilla, L., & Daniel, M. F. (2013). Improving Emotion Comprehension and Social Skills in Early Childhood Through Philosophy for Children. *Childhood & Philosophy, 9*(17), 63–89.

Fair, F., Haas, L. E., Gardosik, C., Johnson, D., Price, D., & Leipnik, O. (2015a). Socrates in the Schools: Gains at Three-year Follow-up. *Journal of Philosophy in Schools, 2*(2).

Fair, F., Haas, L. E., Gardosik, C., Johnson, D. D., Price, D. P., & Leipnik, O. (2015b). Socrates in the Schools From Scotland to Texas: Replicating a Study on the Effects of a Philosophy for Children Program. *Journal of Philosophy in Schools, 2*(1).

García-Moriyón, F., Rebollo, I., & Colom, R. (2005). Evaluating Philosophy for Children. *Thinking: The journal of philosophy for children, 17*(4), 14–22.

Gorard, S., Siddiqui, N., & Huat See, B. (2015). Philosophy for Children: Evaluation Report and Executive Summary. *Education Endowment Foundation, Millbank, UK.*

Hidi, S., Renninger, K. A., & Krapp, A. (2004). Interest, A Motivational Variable That Combines Affective and Cognitive Functioning. *Motivation, Emotion, and Cognition: Integrative Perspectives on Intellectual Functioning and Development,* 89–115.

Lam, C.-M. (2012). Continuing Lipman's and Sharp's Pioneering Work on Philosophy for Children: Using Harry to Foster Critical Thinking in Hong Kong Students. *Educational Research and Evaluation, 18*(2), 187–203.

Lipman, M., & Sharp, A. M. (1978). Some Educational Presuppositions of Philosophy for Children. *Oxford Review of Education, 4*(1), 85–90.

Marashi, S. M. (2008). Teaching Philosophy to Children: A New Experience in Iran. *Analytic Teaching, 27*(1), 12–15.

Nia, A. T. (2014). Investigate the Effect the Philosophy for Children Program (p4c) on Reducing Trait Anger in Teens. *Stud, 4*(2), 449–455.

Othman, M., & Hashim, R. (2006). Critical Thinking & Reading Skills. *Thinking: The Journal of Philosophy for Children, 18*(2), 26–34.

Säre, E., Luik, P., & Tulviste, T. (2016). Improving Preschoolers' Reasoning Skills Using the Philosophy for Children Programme. *Trames: A Journal of the Humanities and Social Sciences, 20*(3), 273.

Tok, Ş., & Mazı, A. (2015). The Effect of Stories for Thinking on Reading and Listening Comprehension: A Case Study in Turkey. *Research in Education, 93*(1), 1–18.

Topping, K. J., & Trickey, S. (2007a). Collaborative Philosophical Enquiry for School Children: Cognitive Effects at 10–12 Years. *British Journal of Educational Psychology, 77*(2), 271–288.

Topping, K. J., & Trickey, S. (2007b). Collaborative Philosophical Inquiry for Schoolchildren: Cognitive Gains at 2-year Follow-up. *British Journal of Educational Psychology, 77*(4), 787–796.

Trickey, S., & Topping, K. J. (2004). 'Philosophy for Children': A Systematic Review. *Research Papers in Education, 19*(3), 365–380.

VanVoorhis, C. W., & Morgan, B. L. (2007). Understanding Power and Rules of Thumb for Determining Sample Sizes. *Tutorials in Quantitative Methods for Psychology, 3*(2), 43–50.

Youssef, C. (2014). A Multilevel Investigation into the Effects of the Philosophical Community of Inquiry on 6th Grade Students' Reading Comprehension, Interest in Maths, Self-esteem, Pro-social Behaviours and Emotional Well-being (Doctoral Dissertation). *Queensland University of Technology, Australia.*

About the Contributors

AGGIE SCHOOL OF ATHENS (TEXAS A&M)

Charles Royal Carlson holds a PhD in Philosophy and a master's degree in biology from Texas A&M University. He is a program manager in Public Partnership and Outreach at Texas A&M University and has been a part of Philosophy for Children (P4C) Texas since its inception. He spent five years with a consortium of faculty at Sam Houston State University actively working to get P4C into the curriculum of local schools and has been instrumental in introducing P4C to pre-elementary age kids. His philosophical work is primarily in American pragmatism and philosophy of biology.

Cora Drozd is a master's student in the Media and Communication department at the London School of Economics and Political Science. Her research focuses on online extremism, speech rights, social media discourse, and media literacy campaigns. She graduated summa cum laude with a BA in Philosophy from Texas A&M University, where she aided Dr. Claire Katz in piloting a program for P4C. She has facilitated philosophy discussions for over 250 youth and continues to advocate for philosophy's role in an internet-mediated democracy.

Robert K. Garcia has a PhD from the University of Notre Dame and is an associate professor of philosophy at Baylor University. He primarily works in analytic metaphysics and philosophy of religion. He is the coeditor of *Is*

Goodness Without God Good Enough? and is currently working on a book on C. S. Lewis's views about the uniqueness of persons. For more information visit www.robertkgarcia.com.

Claire Elise Katz is Murray and Celeste Fasken Chair in Distinguished Teaching and professor of Philosophy at Texas A&M University where she also serves as an associate dean of faculties. She is the founder and director of the Aggie School of Athens, Philosophy Camp for Teens, and the P4C Texas program at Texas A&M University. She teaches and conducts research at the intersection of gender, Judaism, philosophy, and education. She is the author of *Levinas, Judaism, and the Feminine: The Silent Footsteps of Rebecca* (Indiana 2003), *Levinas and the Crisis of Humanism* (Indiana 2013), and *An Introduction to Modern Jewish Philosophy* (I.B. Tauris, 2014). She is the editor with Laura Trout of *Emmanuel Levinas: Critical Assessments* (Routledge 2005) and of *Growing Up with Philosophy Camp: How Thinking Develops Friendship, Community, and a Sense of Self* (Rowman & Littlefield, 2020). She is a 2019 recipient of the Texas A&M University Association of Former Students' University Distinguished Achievement Award for Teaching (University Level) and the American Philosophical Association Prize for Teaching Excellence. In fall 2020, she was named a Presidential Professor for Teaching Excellence (Texas A&M).

Ana Olivares-McFadden is currently a kindergarten dual-language teacher in North Texas. She holds a MA in philosophy with a focus on philosophy of education, which informs her pedagogical approach with early childhood English language learners. Her contribution to this volume was a lesson she conducted at the 2016 Philosophy Camp for Teens.

Michael Portal is a doctoral student in the Department of Philosophy at Texas A&M University (United States). He studies contemporary phenomenology and hermeneutics. His work concerns memory and its limits, and how the past can haunt the present. He is the assistant editor for *Arendt Studies: A Journal for Research on the Life, Work, and Legacy of Hannah Arendt*.

Roger Sansom received undergraduate degrees at Victoria University of Wellington, New Zealand, before doing his PhD in philosophy at The University of North Carolina at Chapel Hill. He does research in philosophy of science and philosophy of biology. His book, *Ingenious Genes* (MIT Press

2011), proposes that the way gene expression is regulated by other genes is in a crucial respect like the way neurons activate each other in the brain. The feature that allows brains to learn allows gene regulation to evolve by natural selection to control each organism's development.

Lynne Masel Walters, PhD, is a senior associate professor in the Department of Teaching, Learning and Culture at Texas A&M University. Her teaching and research interests are in multicultural education and the ways to increase reflective and critical thinking and technological competence by preservice teachers. She also teaches and studies the use of digital storytelling in K-16 classrooms. Dr. Walters received her doctoral degree from the University of Wisconsin-Madison.

Chia-Chiang Wang is an assistant professor at the Department of Counseling, School, and Educational Psychology, the State University of New York at Buffalo. He received his PhD degree in rehabilitation counseling and psychology with a minor in educational psychology from the University of Wisconsin-Madison in 2011. He also earned a master's degree in health care services and outcomes research from Northwestern University during his postdoctoral research fellowship there. He has conducted several meta-analysis studies on educational and psychotherapy outcomes. One of his research interests is to examine the overall effectiveness of educational and psychological interventions and evidence-based practices.

Zhuoying Wang is a PhD student in the Department of Educational Psychology, Center for Research & Development in Dual Language & Literacy Acquisition in the College of Education and Human Development, Texas A&M University. Her research interests include assessment and evaluation for English learners in ESL and bilingual settings, as well as examining their self-regulated learning motivation and strategies.

Sijin Yan is a doctoral student in the Department of Teaching, Learning, and Culture at Texas A&M University, College Station. Her areas of interest center around the philosophy of education, P4C, hermeneutic phenomenology, gender theory, and ethics. In addition to her research, she teaches multicultural education classes, and practices and engages in conversation about P4C on a regular basis.

CORRUPT THE YOUTH (AUSTIN, TEXAS)

Alex Hargroder was a high school teacher and administrator in Louisiana and Texas before joining the Scheller Teacher Education Program at MIT as a project-based learning coach and designer. He trains teachers in progressive and interdisciplinary methodologies, with a special focus on reflective practices, equity, and the socio-emotional dimensions of learning. Alex is a founding board member of Corrupt the Youth, a philosophy outreach program.

Briana Toole is an assistant professor of Philosophy at Claremont McKenna College. Her research, which lies at the intersection of epistemology, feminist philosophy, and critical race theory, has been featured in *Hypatia* and *Episteme*. Briana is the founder and executive director of Corrupt the Youth.

IOWA LYCEUM (UNIVERSITY OF IOWA)

Landon D. C. Elkind was previously an Iowa Lyceum organizer and its president for three years. He started in philosophy as a pre-college student himself, by solo reading Plato's *Republic* on a family road trip to Houston when he was in junior high. He coedited the 2018 collection of essays, *The Philosophy of Logical Atomism: A Centenary Celebration*. He has published on word choice in mathematical practice, logical atomsim and modality, and Buddhist criticisms of Jain theories of self. He received a 2019 Travel Award from the *Journal of the History of Philosophy*, a 2018 Research Travel Grant from McMaster University, and a 2016 Outstanding Teaching Award from the University of Iowa. He is currently a visiting assistant professor at the University of Iowa and also treasurer of the Bertrand Russell Society and Society for the Study of the History of Analytical Philosophy.

Gregory Stoutenburg is a visiting assistant professor of Philosophy at York College of Pennsylvania. He cofounded the Iowa Lyceum while a graduate student at the University of Iowa, where he earned his PhD in Philosophy. Gregory has published numerous journal articles in philosophy, especially in epistemology, where his interests center on skepticism and the uses of knowledge-talk. He now directs a philosophy club at a local high school.

SALISBURY UNIVERSITY (SU)

Cristina Cammarano is associate professor of Philosophy at Salisbury University (SU) where she also leads a program of philosophy in schools. She enjoys thinking about the role of philosophy in the education of human persons and communities. She received her PhD in Philosophy and Education at Teachers College, Columbia University, and was a high school teacher of Philosophy and History in Italy before immigrating to the United States for graduate school.

Kimberly Arriaga-Gonzalez is an undergraduate student at SU where she studies English and Philosophy. She likes to think about philosophy's importance within different cultural spaces. She spends time with the Latinx community and hopes to open more discussions about philosophy in her community.

Jackson Malkus graduated from SU with a Bachelor's degree in philosophy. He enjoys questioning conventional models of teaching and learning and is particularly interested in exploring the role that philosophical discussion can play in K–12 education. He plans to continue his education in philosophy and become a professional teacher.

UNIVERSITY OF KENTUCKY (UK)

Caroline Buchanan earned her PhD at the University of Kentucky (UK) and is a clinical ethics consultant and ethics educator for medical students, residents, fellows, and undergraduates at the UK. Her research specializes in German philosophy, feminist theory, and social and political philosophy. She studies definitions of personhood, research ethics, and organizational ethics in medical education and hospital settings.

Suraj Chaudhary is a PhD candidate in Philosophy at the UK, specializing in philosophy of space and place, phenomenology, and philosophy of technology.

Lauren K. O'Dell is a PhD student at the UK specializing in health care ethics and feminist analytic philosophy.

Clay Graham is a PhD candidate in Philosophy at the UK. He specializes in early modern philosophy and also works in a number of applied ethical fields, including food ethics and health care ethics.

James William Lincoln is a PhD Candidate in Philosophy and an affiliate student in the Center for Equality and Social Justice at the UK specializing in ethics, epistemology, and social philosophy. His research focuses on moral perception and he serves as national secretary for the Society of Philosophers in America.

Andrew Van't Land is a PhD Student in Philosophy at the UK. He studies ancient and contemporary social and political philosophy, examining the complex influence of Aristotle on Marxist feminism's economic and ethical analyses of "the working condition."

Colin Smith is a PhD Candidate in Philosophy at the UK specializing in ancient philosophy.

PHILOSOPHY AND CRITICAL THINKING (PACT)—OHIO STATE

Justin D'Arms is professor of Philosophy at Ohio State University. He was department chair as Philosophy and Critical Thinking (PACT) was launched and was in charge of the budget and the pursuit of grants for the program. His work in philosophy focuses on ethics and moral psychology.

James Fritz is term assistant professor of Philosophy at Virginia Commonwealth University. He earned his PhD in philosophy at the Ohio State

University, where he was the founding lead instructor for PACT. He has also taught philosophy at the elementary school and undergraduate levels. James's philosophical research is primarily concerned with connections between ethics and epistemology.

Julia Jorati is associate professor of philosophy at the University of Massachusetts Amherst. She is a cofounder of the PACT summer camp for high school students at Ohio State and directed it for three years. In addition to teaching pre-college and college students, she likes to read and write about early modern philosophy.

Lavender McKittrick-Sweitzer is a philosophy PhD candidate at Ohio State University. She had served as an instructor of the Ohio State PACT Summer Camp since its beginning in 2017. Her primary research interests are at the intersection of political and feminist philosophy. Lavender is passionate about making philosophy accessible to all.

WESTERN MICHIGAN LYCEUM

Charlie Kurth is an associate professor in the Western Michigan University philosophy department. His research explores questions at the intersection of ethics, moral psychology, and emotion theory. He recently published *The Anxious Mind: An Investigation of the Varieties and Virtues of Anxiety* (MIT Press, 2018) and has placed articles in journals like *Ethics*, *Philosophy of Science*, *Mind & Language*, and *Philosophical Studies*. He also serves as the faculty adviser for the Western Michigan Lyceum.

Adam Waggoner is a graduate student in the University of Michigan philosophy department, where he works in ancient Greek philosophy and value theory. Prior to coming to the University of Michigan, he received his MA in Philosophy at Western Michigan University and helped direct the 2019 WMU Lyceum. At Michigan, he continues to pursue his interests in pre-college philosophy as an ethics bowl coach and facilitator of the philosophy with Kids program, which aims to bring philosophy into elementary school classrooms.

www.ingramcontent.com/pod-product-compliance
Lightning Source LLC
Chambersburg PA
CBHW052043300426
44117CB00012B/1944